Comparing Public
Bureaucracies

Comparing Public Bureaucracies

Problems of Theory and Method

B. Guy Peters

The University of Alabama Press
Tuscaloosa • London

Library of Congress Cataloging-in-Publication Data

Peters, B. Guy.
Comparing public bureaucracies.

Bibliography: p.
Includes index.
1. Bureaucracy. 2. Public administration.
3. Comparative government. I. Title.
JF1501.P435 1988   350'.001   87-5077
ISBN 0-8173-0368-5
ISBN 0-8173-0384-7 (pbk.)

British Library Cataloguing-in-Publication Data is available.

In memory of SDA and RCMcD

Contents

Tables

Tables

Figures

Preface

This book began its life as the 1986 Coleman B. Ransone Lectures in Public Administration and Policy at the University of Alabama, a lecture series inaugurated in the mid-1940s. I felt honored to be invited to give the lectures and to follow in the footsteps of the many distinguished previous lecturers. The opportunity was especially welcome because it gave me the occasion (and the need) to ponder a number of aspects of comparative public administration about which my thinking was at best disorganized and inchoate at the outset of writing. I hope that by the time these thoughts reach the printed page they will seem clear and will be meaningful to other readers.

When these lectures were first conceived, they were to focus on public administration in the United States and then to discuss what makes American public bureaucracy distinctive when compared with that in other industrialized societies. As I began to think through the problems, however, more important theoretical and intellectual issues presented themselves. Consequently this book is now much less about the practice of government in the United States than about the apparent decline in the study of comparative public administration. This field of inquiry in political science once displayed great promise and for some time made great strides. It is now the concern of relatively few scholars, however, and has become mired in endless descriptive studies of rather minute aspects of administrative structure or behavior in single countries, with little theoretical and conceptual development. Some readers may consider such an appraisal excessive, and I do apologize in advance if it causes offense. I believe, however, that it is justified by the evidence, some of which I present herein. The comparative study of public bureaucracy is indeed now seen very much through a darkened glass. What accounts for this decline in intellectual fortunes and change in intellectual fashions?

This book will provide some answers to the question and more important will indicate some avenues of escape from the doldrums. In particular, I will focus on the development of empirical measures that will allow comparative public administration to conform to the usual standards of scholarship in the contemporary social sciences. I will then return to focus once again on the United States because of the relatively great availability of data and the relative familiarity of the author with that data. In each instance, however, I will present some comparative data. Despite the concentration of data sources, I intend the arguments presented about both the study of public administration and public administration itself to be generic. The reader will, however, notice that the majority of literature and examples cited are drawn from industrialized democracies, again because of the interests and limited expertise of the author.

Several people deserve special thanks for assistance in the development and preparation of the book. First, those at the University of Alabama who attended the lectures for four days deserve praise for their patience, for their persistence, and not least for their many interesting and useful comments. Several of my colleagues at the University of Pittsburgh, most notably William Dunn, Bert Rockman, and Roger Benjamin, provided helpful comments on parts of the manuscript. I owe a special thanks to William Gormley of the University of Wisconsin, who, while on a Mellon Postdoctoral Fellowship at the University of Pittsburgh, provided extremely useful and constructive comments on the entire book. Patricia Ingraham of the Maxwell School provided comments and a much needed source of information at the Office of Personnel Management as well as general encouragement. Beauregard says thanks. My good friend and collaborator Martin Heisler of the University of Maryland also provided much needed information in the nick of time. Scholars in the International Political Science Association Study Group on the Structure and Organization of Government, which I am fortunate enough to co-chair, have heard in preliminary form many of the ideas elaborated here. They provided useful comments at several conferences. Brian W. Hogwood of the Department of Politics, University of Strathclyde, helped me develop much of my thinking about organizational change and is coauthor of chapter 3. The research reported in that chapter was assisted by a grant from the National Science Foundation (SES 83-08161).

Two anonymous reviewers also helped to improve the manuscript. One in particular showed unusual intellectual openness. He or she disagreed in a very fundamental way about several points made here but evaluated the book on its merits.

On a more personal level, I express my appreciation to Victor Gibean, Frank Blitz, Philip Coulter, Joseph Pilegge, and all the other members of the Political Science Department at the University of Alabama who made my stay in Tuscaloosa pleasant and rewarding. I was especially saddened to hear of the passing of Coleman Ransone, for whom the lecture series was named. He showed me great kindness in Tuscaloosa. It is a pleasure to have known him. Sandra Mathews as usual provided skillful secretarial assistance and tried (usually unsuccessfully) to keep me organized. Michael Feigenbaum provided some much needed research assistance, and an extremely helpful public employee at the Embassy of Canada helped me answer a few important questions. My family bore the burden when I spent too many days at the office writing and was grumpy because the words were not coming as they should.

Comparing Public Bureaucracies

1

The Need for Comparison
in Public Bureaucracy
and the Difficulties Involved

We all have a tendency to conceptualize politics or economics or culture in terms of our own national or even personal experiences. This statement may be especially true of the social sciences in the United States. Contemporary social science theory has had a disproportionate share of its development in the United States, and American values and experiences have been projected on the rest of the world. If we are to develop meaningful theoretical perspectives in the social sciences, however, we must examine each national experience in light of that of other nations. In so doing we will be able to investigate the ways in which differences in structures, cultures, and values affect each other and the performance of the particular aspect of the social system that is being investigated.

The tendency to extrapolate and develop theory on the basis of a single national experience is perhaps especially evident in the administrative experience and public bureaucracy of the United States. Much of our discussion of public administration (not only for the United States but for much of the rest of the world) has been very much bound to a particular time and place. The result has been rather unfortunate for theory development concerning public administration as a component of the social sciences inasmuch as we have almost nothing approaching a paradigm for the study of public administration, especially if we demand a paradigm useful outside Washington, D.C., the United States, or more generally the industrialized world (Lundquist, 1985). While a single paradigm may not be necessary or even desirable, the absence of any successful and

1

broadly shared attempts to develop comprehensive approaches represents a major weakness in the theoretical development of this field of inquiry. The several attempts made (Frederickson, 1980; see also Wollmann, 1980) seem driven more by normative concerns than by the need to understand public administration in a broader comparative and theoretical perspective.

This short book is certainly not intended to articulate an overarching paradigm for public administration, although I hope that it takes a step in the right direction. In these pages I intend rather to examine several major aspects of public administration in the United States in a more comparative and theoretically motivated manner than writers have usually done in the past. Several of the essays contained in this volume represent efforts to articulate partial theories, at least, relating to a particular aspect of administration. I hope that together they will at a minimum push back some of the barriers which have inhibited development of a more comprehensive understanding of public administration. In other words these chapters are attempts at middle-range or institutional theories which may be able to mediate between any evolving paradigm in the field and newly discovered empirical generalizations and experiences.

The Purposes of Comparative Public Administration

In some ways the need to justify and defend the practice of comparative public administration attests to the incomplete conquest of political science, and especially public administration, by those concerned with the development of meaningful social theory. It is almost certainly trite to argue that theory in the social sciences proceeds largely by comparison or by the development of abstract concepts (such as Weber's ideal types), against which elements of the real world should be compared. To regard comparative public administration as somehow distinct from public administration, or indeed to consider comparative politics distinct from the study of politics more generally, is to be trapped in the "stamps, flags, and coins"

2

school of comparative politics and comparative administration. That is, comparative public administration has been viewed as a series of excursions into the exotica of world political systems with the intention of describing different administrative systems and, with any luck, of developing a repertoire of amusing anecdotes based on field work. Such a concept of comparative administration could, however, be justified by much of the literature in the field, which has been descriptive and based on a single country without seeking to provide broader conceptual and theoretical perspectives (Ridley, 1979; Rowat, 1984; Tummala, 1982; but see Page, 1985; Peters, 1984). As Riggs once wrote, "inevitably a new framework for 'comparative' administration will evolve—not as a 'subfield' but as the master field within which 'American public administration' will be a subfield" (1976:652).

While Riggs was perhaps excessively optimistic, the direction to which he pointed would certainly be the one offering the opportunity for the greatest theoretical development. Significant work in the philosophy of social science and the methodology of empirical research shows that a strategy of triangulation—using two or more approaches within two or more contexts—is practically the only way to separate the theoretical and cultural bias of the observer from actual observations in the field (Campbell, 1975). Observers impose any number of biases when they observe, and the observation of any complex social phenomenon such as public administration is especially prone to such biases. It is therefore crucial for theoretical development to foster more and better comparative studies. How, then, should we proceed with the task of comparison? It will be important to define at least four dimensions.

Cross-national Comparisons

As indicated by my statements above, I view comparative administration as more than simply the accumulation of descriptive material about various different countries. In particular, I do not have in mind the presentation of such material on a country-by-country basis. Such description is sometimes useful as a means of beginning a more theoretical inquiry. It is certainly pedagogically important for students who may not know a *Beamte* from an *ENArque*. Countries as nominal categories for describing systems of public administration, however, may not offer the most efficient means of understanding *why* those systems function as they do. The extremely fragmented form taken by the policymaking of the public bureaucracy in the United States, for example, has little or nothing to do with national character per se (except as it reflects the fear of strong central government at the time when the Republic was founded). The fragmentation has a great deal more to do with the structure of the governing institutions— both bureaucratic and political—which have been developed within the constitutional framework. At times there may of course be patterns which are more readily explained by cultural variables, for example possibly the legalism of public administration in West Germany. Until we begin to move away from the country-centric approach to comparative administration, however, it will be difficult to ascertain which patterns of behavior are peculiarly national (see also Halász, 1985).

It may be especially important to attempt to understand public administration—and indeed government more broadly—in the United States in a comparative context. Much of the thinking about public administration which by now has become pervasive worldwide—that of Gulick and Urwick, Simon, March, Lindblom, Waldo, Wildavsky, Mosher, and so on—is American in origin, and to some extent the professional study of public administration is therefore extremely culture bound, even when it is conducted outside the United States. For example, a major British book on public administration theory (Self, 1972) concentrates very heavily on American rather than British sources. Such approaches to administration are ethnocentric not just because of their origins (the genetic fallacy) but because the constructs, hypotheses, and theories are not necessarily representative of reality (valid) in other political and cultural contexts. There is thus a pressing need to regard the United States as one of many industrialized capitalist democracies and to recognize the uniqueness of the system but at the same time to acknowledge that it shows many points of similarity to other political systems (Bodiguel, 1984). Before we can do so, however, we must develop a set of research questions and a set of categories which can be used for comparison. In the following chapters I intend to take a first step toward the development of a broader comparative perspective on public bureaucracy in the United States as well as to make a statement about the conduct of the enterprise of comparative public administration. At a very minimum, I will present a selection of dependent variables which will be useful in the process of comparison across nations.

Cross-time Comparisons

In addition to the obvious comparisons to be made across political systems, useful comparisons of administrative systems can be done across time within single countries (Benjamin, 1982; Gladden, 1972). Some very important insights into the nature of public bureaucracy have been gained by studying bureaucracies and political systems which vanished centuries ago (Eisenstadt, 1963; Wittfogel, 1957) or by studying bureaucracies at earlier stages of development within currently existing political systems (Armstrong, 1973; Chapman, 1984; Lipset, 1963; Parris, 1969). Again, however, such analysis needs to be conducted within the context of an analytic framework which provides the compilation of the historical data with some meaning. It could be argued that the public bureaucracy is especially well suited to such informed historical analysis, as it has been an identifiable institution longer than other institutions associated with contemporary government (especially contemporary political democracies). In addition, the public bureaucracy continues to perform most of the functions which it has performed historically while adding new functions and perhaps increasing its importance in policymaking (Molitor, 1983). As a result we have a set of structures that have been identifiable for a long period of time and can be examined in terms of roles and behaviors within the process of governing. There is also some possibility of determining to what extent variance (if such "hard" statistical language is not inappropriate for research which would necessarily be more qualitative) can be explained by national attributes and to what extent by levels of development, by the tasks being performed, or by the climate of ideas popular at the particular time. This exercise in turn might provide some insight into the problems encountered in studying contemporary bureaucracies created by diffusion and "Galton's Problem" (Klingman, 1980). Although such careful historical research is certainly desirable, like all comparative research into public bureaucracies, it must overcome a number of serious conceptual and methodological roadblocks which I will discuss here and in the chapters that follow.

Cross-level Comparisons

Another way of attempting to isolate the sources of variance in the role and behavior of public bureaucracies is to perform comparisons across levels of government within single countries. When we speak of "the bureaucracy" in the United States, we tend to think of the federal government and to forget the almost 83,000 other governments which exist in the country, most of which have employees and therefore have something which we can loosely call a bureaucracy. Comparisons within a single country can be especially important for exercises in theory building because one of the variables assumed to influence behavior—political culture, national character, or whatever one wishes to call it—is held constant (unless of course there are significant regional differences within the single country). A number of other factors which may influence behavior, however, do tend to vary significantly. In the United States, for example, a large number of the 83,000 governments are special districts performing functions which are at least in principle marketable and for which there may be available substitute goods in the private sector. Does the twin account-

ability to the marketplace and to political officials (Lane, 1985;
Rose 1985b) affect the manner in which these public employees perform their tasks? Do variations in governmental
structures, or even simply the size of governments, affect the
behavior of public employees? A number of excellent opportunities for research in public administration comparing levels
of government have yet to be fully explored. Furthermore,
these lower levels of government could be involved in more
complex research designs (diagonal or matrix comparisons)
which could be used to help isolate the source of "variance" in
observations. Again, in view of the relatively low level of theoretical development in comparative administration, even
thinking about such opportunities may be premature, but they
are nevertheless intriguing.

Cross-policy Comparisons

Finally, it is important to compare administration across a
number of different policy areas. Some of the functions which
government performs (delivering the mails or delivering babies)
are very similar to the functions performed in the private sector. Others (delivering bombs) are more strictly governmental.
Some government functions require direct interaction between
a public employee; others can be performed simply with laws,
regulations, or even information (Hood, 1986). Some government functions require the services of highly qualified professionals, such as physicians and lawyers, while others may be
performed by employees with only a minimal education. These
characteristics of different programs and policies may substantially affect the manner in which they are organized and the
behavior of individuals within the organizations.

It is important to compare administration across functions,
but just as in the case of comparisons across countries, it is
important to use something other than nominal categories
when classifying the functions. There may be as much variance within a category such as "health" as there is between
some aspects of health and, for example, some parts of educa-

tion. An important aspect of theoretical development in the study of public administration, therefore, is the development of theoretically meaningful classification schemes. To some extent such schemes have already begun to be developed through various contingency approaches to administration (Greenwood, Hinings, and Ranson, 1975a; 1975b; Pitt and Smith, 1981). Such development apparently has a very long way to go, however, especially if we want to be able to use the schemes when we design new government institutions and not just when we describe the characteristics of existing institutions.

The Low Level of Development of Comparative Administration

Having recognized the importance of comparison for the development of our thinking about public administration, we now come to the awful truth that the comparative study of public administration is perhaps the least well developed aspect of the study of comparative politics and government despite the long and honorable history of the field. Comparative administration was a central component in the traditional approaches to comparative government. Many of the classic textbooks in the field of comparative government included extensive sections on administration and the execution of law through the public bureaucracy. The comparative study of public bureaucracy also occupied a central place in development studies in the 1950s, 1960s, and 1970s as scholars attempted to understand the role of the bureaucracy in implementing development programs as well as differences in administrative behavior related to levels of development (LaPalombara, 1963; Riggs, 1964; Siffin, 1971; Heady, 1979, provides a thorough overview of the development administration literature). As Savage (1976) observed, however, comparative administration "started with no paradigm of its own and developed none" (p. 417). This statement is to some extent true for public administration as a whole, but its validity is especially evident in comparative administration because of the close connections with comparative politics.

Although it made a strong beginning and showed great promise, the comparative study of public administration has waned (see Lundquist, 1985). It is perhaps especially instructive that, although the comparative study of public policy began explicitly as a "subfield" within academic political science much later than comparative administration, in the eyes of most people (I believe) it has made greater progress than has comparative administration, especially if progress is measured by the canons of normal social science (Hancock, 1983). Any number of models and theories have been developed to explain differences in policy, and at least some of these models have been subjected to empirical testing (Bunce, 1984; Flora and Heidenheimer, 1981; Heidenheimer, Heclo, and Adams, 1984; Lehner, 1985; Leichter, 1979). The same can certainly not be said of the comparative study of public administration, an area in which few, if any, rigorous models have been developed and fewer have been tested empirically (but see Aberbach, Putnam, and Rockman, 1981). It is indeed rather amusing now to reread the rosy predictions about the developments in this field that were published in the 1960s and 1970s, including the arguments that comparative public policy studies were a virgin field for exploration by students of comparative administration (Jun, 1976). I am afraid that it would be fair to say that some intellectual malaise has attached to comparative administration.

Why should there be such malaise in such an important area? The material for comparative study is certainly rich. As noted above, the public bureaucracy is perhaps the easiest of the major political institutions to study comparatively because its structures are relatively identifiable and the activities carried out within it relatively uniform. There are, of course, some interesting and important variations on this presumed identifiability and uniformity, perhaps the most important being the increasing use of "third-party government" to exercise many nominally governmental functions (Salamon, 1981a; Sharkansky, 1979). When one knocks on doors, however, one is likely to see more similarities in bureaucratic offices than in legislators' offices (Kornberg, 1973) or even in the offices of chief executives (Rose and Suleiman, 1980).

One reason for the malaise in the study of comparative administration is the potential argument, in line with one important approach to this field, that there is little or nothing to compare and that the uniformity will be found to be overwhelming. If one accepts the logic of Weberian and/or Wilsonian approaches to public administration, one may be tempted to say first that all public organizations will, over time, tend toward the bureaucratic form (but see Page, 1985). Even if public bureaucracies were differently structured and organized, however, they would be uninteresting because the public bureaucrat is involved not in politics but in the "mere execution of the laws." As Gray and Jenkins (1985) noted, "Administrative behavior was viewed as either unimportant or unproblematic (or both)" (p. 23).

Such a statement may appear to come perilously close to the old dichotomy between politics and administration. Although this dichotomy has presumably been debunked, it is important to remember how durable it is and how long it has lasted (Campbell and Peters, forthcoming; Ingraham and Ban, 1986), especially for those who participate in government. The dichotomy may be equally durable for some scholars who work on other political institutions such as the presidency and who assume that members of the bureaucracy are indeed supposed to accept the legitimate orders of the president. Concern for the proper execution of the law has to some degree entered the study of public administration through the back door in the guise of implementation studies (Barrett and Fudge, 1981; Grindle, 1980; Pressman and Wildavsky, 1973). Failures to achieve policy goals are frequently blamed on the recalcitrance of the public bureaucracy rather than on any inherent weaknesses in the legislation which was enacted (Linder and Peters, forthcoming). In general, the assumption appears to be that, if the civil service behaved as it should, then government might be able to function properly as well.

In addition to the problems with the dichotomy between pol-

10

itics and administration, there are significant problems with the assumption that public organizations will tend toward bureaucratic principles. If we examine the structure and functioning of organizations in the federal government we can find some organizations, for example in the executive office of the president, which might closely resemble patrimonial organizations: the members are personally loyal to the leader and come and go at his or her pleasure. Also, an increasing number of organizations, for example in areas such as health or legal services, might be organized around professional rather than hierarchical values. We would expect a declining number of organizations to approach the more rigid structure expected in a bureaucratic organization. We are less certain, however, about the way in which differences in structures translate directly into differences in the behavior of the members of the organization or in the outputs of the organization. There is a good deal of evidence regarding such relationships for private sector organizations but substantially less for public sector organizations.

Another reason, closely related to the first, why comparative public administration appears not to have made the strides seen in some other aspects of comparative politics is the training in the study of politics which many people received during the "behavioral revolution." To a great extent comparative administration, and to some degree the study of all political institutions, were denigrated, while greater emphasis was placed on the study of "inputs" into the political process, such as voting, attitudes, and socialization. Functional approaches to comparative politics largely condemned the institutions of government to a "black box" which was deemed to be an uninteresting place to explore.

Perhaps I exaggerate, but there was certainly some overreaction to the traditional dominance of formal institutional studies in the comparative politics prior to this revolution. In fairness, some of the overreaction is now being corrected in the course of the resurgence of institutional analysis in political science (March and Olsen, 1984; Peters, 1985a). In addition, the burgeoning interest in the concept of the state (Benjamin and

Elkin, 1985; Dyson, 1980) may, as it develops, require more attention to be paid to political institutions such as the public bureaucracy. Much must still be done, however, to develop approaches to comparative public administration which will be fully respectable to other colleagues in the social sciences while still capturing the nuanced interpretations that are necessary for an understanding of the operations of the modern bureaucracies and their roles in making public policy.

Still another factor affecting the development of the study of comparative public administration has been the emergence of policy studies and the growing concern with issues of public policy. As a part of the "postbehavioral revolution" this development was, on the output side of the black box of government, what the behavioral revolution was for the input side. That is, when attention was directed toward outputs and outcomes of government action, we lost sight of much that was involved in making policy. In part, the loss took place in the rush to quantify during the study of public policy. Politics became the readily quantifiable indicators of partisanship, with perhaps a few institutional factors thrown in; the subtleties of process were largely ignored. Not very surprisingly, many of the early analyses found that "politics doesn't matter" (Dye, 1966; Hofferbert, 1966; but see Sharkansky 1967). In light of these findings, then, it appeared reasonable to disregard or to denigrate the role of politics—especially the very subtle politics that may occur within complex political institutions—when attempting to understand public policy.

The comparative study of public policy was able to stamp out, or at least to imperil, the comparative study of public administration in part because of the presumed greater ease of measurement and hence the appearance of greater "scientific" rigor. In public expenditures there was a ready-made ratio level measure which (at least presumably) could be used in any and all political systems (but see Peters and Heisler, 1983). Other indicators that were seemingly also ready-made were available for measuring not only government expenditures for a particular purpose but some of the actual impacts of government programs on social and economic conditions. These included

12

infant mortality for health care and the number of recipients for social welfare policy. These available indicators gave the study of policy a decided advantage over the study of administration, which had fewer indicators and fewer still agreed-upon indicators (see below): the study of policy could be made to appear more scientific. Scholars in the public policy component of the discipline of political science could publish in the "mainstream" journals, while those interested in public administration, and especially in comparative administration, found it much more difficult to do so (but see Meier, 1975; Muramatsu and Krauss, 1984).

In addition, the policy approach had the advantage of being inclusive and to some extent could encompass much of the research which was being done in public administration (Lundquist, 1985). It did so primarily under the rubric of implementation studies, which in many ways represented old public administration in new bottles (Hood, 1976). Also associated with the policy studies movement have been terms such as *political economy* (which means a variety of things in a variety of different settings) that have also been quite inclusive and have diverted attention from more traditional inquiry into public administration questions.

To this point, I have been somewhat indiscriminately spreading the blame for the rather underdeveloped nature of comparative public administration. While it is admittedly more difficult to develop a rigorous approach to comparative public administration, the necessary developments have plainly not as yet taken place. How could comparative public administration be made more a component of "mainstream" political science?

Perhaps the first and most fundamental problem facing the comparative study of public administration is the absence of any agreement as to what we are studying—as to what, in the language of the social sciences, constitutes the dependent variable. Even other institutions in government have readily available dependent variables, such as voting in legislatures and decisions in the courts, which have enabled them to use "modern" social science techniques.

13

At least four possible candidates—or really sets of candidates—might have the honor of being dependent variables in the study of public administration. All are important, and indeed no one should be chosen to the exclusion of the others. We need, however, to consider the manner in which concentration on one or another of them will direct the development of our theoretical basis for understanding public bureaucracies. Furthermore, it is necessary to regard these sets of characteristics of administrative systems more explicitly in terms of variables. The terms themselves are hardly new, but we should approach them in a way that will permit greater theoretical development.

We might, for example, view public administration as a set of people who happen to be public employees. This statement may appear rather trivial, but by simply looking at the people who work for government we can tell a good deal about how the administrative system will function. In the first place, it would be nice to know how many people work for government. The number is by no means easy to determine, even for advanced industrial societies with well-developed systems of record keeping and detailed statements of personnel policy (Martin, 1982; Rose et al., 1985). The most fundamental prerequisite is an operational definition of a public employee, which is becoming increasingly difficult to articulate (Peters, 1986c; Rein, 1985).

In addition to simply knowing the relative size of public bureaucracies in a number of countries, knowledge of the number of public employees is important for assessing the administrative capacity of government and for understanding the relationship between state and society, especially in a period of concern about big government (Peters and Heisler, 1983). In addition, some approaches to policymaking have stressed that the public bureaucracy plays a central role in developing and diffusing new policy ideas (Heclo, 1974). Finally, when such numerical information is combined with information about the pay and perquisites of public employment, we can gain some insight into the place of public servants in society and in their claims to be an elite body. In many Third World countries, for example, the average wage of a central government employee is much greater than average per capita income; it is more than fifteen times average income in Burundi and almost ten times average income in Senegal (Heller and Tait, 1983). In some industrialized countries (for example, Austria) the average wage for central government employees is only very slightly greater than the average income. These figures can give an approximate picture of the status of public employees in a society, although they by no means offer a complete picture.

If we turn to the question of the nature of government personnel, we find that "representative bureaucracy" has a long and honorable history in the study of public bureaucracies (Gboyega, 1984; Kingsley, 1944; Meier, 1975; Putnam, 1976). In general, this literature has examined the social backgrounds— parental social class, education, race, gender, language, and so on—of civil servants and other elites. The vast majority of this literature has concentrated on recruitment for senior, decisionmaking posts in the civil service rather than on recruitment for the entire civil service and has tended to find that the posts are filled primarily by well-educated males from middle-class backgrounds and from the dominant social groupings in the society. This finding is hardly surprising, since leadership positions in both the public and private sectors tend to be filled by people with the same characteristics.

The concern with patterns of recruitment, in addition to being intrinsically interesting, may also be hypothesized to affect patterns of decisionmaking by civil servants, a hypothesis which Putnam (1976) called "plausible, but ambiguous and unsubstantiated" (p. 44). There is, however, more evidence that other background characteristics, such as professional training, have some impact on behavior (Gormley, 1983). In addition to affecting patterns of decisionmaking by top elites, the representatives of the civil service may be important (and more important) in determining the ability of the lower echelons of the service to work with the various clients in the society and in projecting an image of the civil service as truly national. The lower, "street-level" civil servants actually have daily contact with citizens; they project an image of the civil service. The

15

makeup of this group may therefore be more important than the composition of those in the upper echelons.

The question of the representativeness of the civil service may be closely linked to the question of the attitudes and values which the civil servants bring with them into their jobs. It has seemed particularly important to investigate the attitudes with which civil servants approach their place in the policymaking process and their relationships with politicians (Aberbach, Putnam, and Rockman, 1981; Anton, 1980; Eldersveld, Kooiman, and van der Tak, 1981; Mellbourn, 1979; Muramatsu and Krauss, 1984). Some scholars have been concerned with the degree of value congruence between citizens and public officials with regard to issues such as political participation, especially within developing democracies (Eldersveld, Jagannadham, and Barnabas, 1968).

Such attitudinal research is extremely important in defining the roles of bureaucrats, but at times the connection with the actual behavior of the civil servants appears remote. We do not as yet have a very clear picture of the extent to which behavior is structured by the routines and constraints of political institutions rather than by the attitudes and values of those who work within them. One might expect (if we could measure influence) to find that certain institutions, for example the Treasury in the United Kingdom (Heclo and Wildavsky, 1974), have greater impact on behavior than do other, "weaker" organizations. The process of learning does not end in childhood, and institutions can have a powerful socializing effect on individuals. At least at present we cannot claim to understand the effects of attitudes on the behavior of civil servants and especially of senior civil servants.

The people who inhabit the institutions of government are therefore important. Understanding some things about them can give us a starting point for understanding the institutions in their entirety. The characteristics of personnel will not, however, afford us complete answers about the ways in which the individuals will function within extremely complex organizations and within "rules of the game," which will affect their performance. To these institutions we must now turn our attention.

The structure of administrative systems is the most frequently manipulated and perhaps the least understood aspect of public administration (Grafton, 1984; March and Olsen, 1983). Since government began, whenever politicians could find nothing else better to do with their time and energy, and whenever they confronted the need to demonstrate concern for a public problem, they reorganized the public bureaucracy. Public administrators themselves have hardly been unwilling to propose and implement reorganizations. At the scholarly level, literally decades of work on public organizations appear to have failed to develop a workable paradigm for understanding these organizations (but see Leemans, 1976).

In the first place, as I mentioned briefly above, we still lack a good way of differentiating public and private organizations. Just what is a *public* organization? We have now seen a number of extended discussions of the number and nature of organizations which exist at the margin of the state (Barker, 1982; Seidman and Gilmour, 1986; Sharkansky, 1979). A clear distinction is needed, however, if we are to understand whether the public nature of an organization affects the behavior of its members. Furthermore, from a more practical standpoint, we need to be able to enforce standards and types of accountability on public organizations different from those that we bring to bear on private.

The second question implicit in our concern about defining public organizations is the definition of a public *organization*. It is, in comparative terms, quite easy to study the federal bureaucracy in the United States, given that there tend to be identifiable organizations, usually established by some legal or administrative act, with a budget and personnel attached to them. Even here, however, an attempt to assess the organization of, for example, the Office of the Secretary of Defense involves acts of faith regarding the definition of an organization or an organizational component. In many European countries, and indeed in most of the world, the structure of government below the level of the department or ministry is fluid and rarely articulated to the extent that it is in the United States. (Contrast, for example, the *Civil Service Yearbook* from the United Kingdom with the *United States Government Man-*

ual.) In addition, beyond and between the more identifiable structures (even in the United States) lie a host of interdepartmental committees, interministerial committees, coordinating committees, and so on which are important in sorting out the details of policy when organizational jurisdictions overlap, as they inevitably do (Bodiguel, 1981). Finally, as some observers interested in the implementation of policy have noted, policies function effectively not because of *the* organization but because of *the sets* of organizations which work together to deliver services or fail to work together (Benson, 1975; Hanf and Scharpf, 1978; Hjern and Porter, 1981). While the students of implementation have made progress in identifying and conceptualizing about such organizational systems, we still have some distance to go before we can use organizational systems adequately in the comparative study of public administration.

Even if we were certain about the universe of organizations that we would like to study, we would possibly still lack the concepts and language to discuss those organizations and particularly to compare them effectively across the several dimensions mentioned at the outset of this chapter. Some efforts have been made in that direction, but their results as yet appear inadequate for the tasks at hand. The Hood and Dunsire (1981) study of the structure of departments in British central government, for example, provided some insight into structural dimensions in these organizations, but the methodology used in some ways obscured as much information as it provided. Also, some work on public organizations based upon a contingency approach (Greenwood, Hinings, and Ranson, 1975a, 1975b; Pitt and Smith, 1981) has noted that "political salience, accountability and uncertainty have significant effects upon the structuring of government organizations." In general, however, structure appears to have been considered a less important characteristic of public bureaucracies than we might have expected, given organizational studies in the private sector and given the historical concern of public administration with structural questions (Gulick and Urwick, 1937).

I argued earlier that attitudes might have a relatively slight impact on bureaucratic behavior, a third possible dependent variable. This dependent variable may be especially difficult to use, especially when the researcher is concerned with the behavior of senior civil servants. Much of their important work is conducted in private, and especially in countries such as the United Kingdom, where there are strong norms about secrecy and privacy, it may be difficult to extract reliable information about "real" behavior. Nevertheless, there are a number of interesting studies of the behavior of civil servants in important decisionmaking politics, most notably the Heclo and Wildavsky (1974) study of the British Treasury, presumably the most secretive of all institutions. Rather than being truly comparative, however, most of this literature comprises studies of decisionmaking within a single country and often focuses on a single policy decision (Good, 1980; Pliatzky, 1982; Porter, 1980; Young and Sloman, 1982, 1984). Like different political systems, different policy areas may have their own patterns of decisionmaking. Colin Campbell's (1983) and Campbell's and George Szablowski's (1979) studies of elite decisionmaking in the United States, the United Kingdom, and Canada are exceptional in being truly comparative.

Some systematic attempts to measure and analyze bureaucratic behavior have of course been made using the reported actions of senior civil servants either while they were in office or after they left. Kvavik (1978), Johansen and Kristensen (1982), and others, for example, have made extensive analyses of the reported behavior of Scandinavian civil servants, especially as they interact with interest group representatives. Suleiman (1974) has collected similar information for French civil servants. Gordon (1971) and Christoph (1975) have less systematically examined the behavior of British civil servants with respect to organized interests. Kaufman (1981b) spent some months actually observing senior civil servants as they went about their daily tasks. Again, however, we lack an explicit comparative framework within which to assess this behavior.

Perhaps not surprisingly, the most formalized and theoretically motivated discussions of bureaucratic behavior have been developed by economists seeking to apply their utility-maximizing paradigm to public bureaucracies (Breton and Wintrobe, 1975; Niskanen, 1971). These models assume that bureaucrats will attempt to maximize the size of their bureaus and will accumulate as many personal perquisites as possible. While this model has been critiqued many times (Jackson, 1982; Kogan, 1973), it may have some relevance for empirical comparative research. Although Hood, Huby, and Dunsire (1984), for example, have applied the model to departments in British central government with disappointing results, the results might be different in a more decentralized and differentiated bureaucracy, such as that of the United States or even Sweden (see chapter 4).

While the study of recruitment of civil servants has concentrated on the upper echelons, it might be useful to focus on the lower echelons when studying bureaucratic behavior. The role of the senior civil servant may be constrained by the political and social mores of the service, and by the delicate relationships with political masters, but the tasks performed in the lower ranks of the civil service may be more similar across political systems and political cultures. We may thus be able to assess the impact of cultural and social variables on behavior better by examining the lower levels, especially where the relationship between clients and civil servants—"street-level bureaucracy"—in different social and political settings is concerned. Some interesting work of this sort has already been carried out and demonstrates substantial differences in interactions (Goodsell, 1981; Katz and Eisenstadt, 1960; Prottas, 1979; Sjoberg, Brymer, and Farris, 1978). In another extremely interesting piece of research, Goodsell (1976) examined patterns of performance in the post offices of the United States and Costa Rica, attempting to determine what effects differences in cultures would have on the performance of the same task and also on patterns of interaction within the organizations. This type of work, rather than merely giving attention to the peaks of power, is apparently likely to illuminate the impact of some of the independent variables—social structure, political culture, and so on—in comparative administration and indeed in comparative politics.

20

Some aspects of bureaucratic behavior are purposive, or directed toward the achievement of some goal external to the organization, while much of the activity is reflexive, or directed toward the maintenance of internal organizational processes and regularities (Mohr, 1973). One of the most important aspects of reflexive behavior in public organizations is the relationship between civil servants and their nominal political masters. As noted above, this question has been subjected to much attitudinal investigation and has also been discussed by those more interested in practical politics than in academic research. Many political appointees in the Reagan administration, for example, have attempted, with the assistance of the Heritage Foundation, to find ways of making the federal bureaucracy more responsive to their own self-proclaimed "radical agenda" (Butler, Sanera, and Weinrod, 1984). "Who Governs?" is a question with a long history. It is still far from being answered finally with respect to the relationship between the civil service and political executives (Hawker, 1981).

To determine the relative power of these two potentially competing sets of actors, we might develop models of their relationships, to some degree as ideal-type models, and then compare real-world systems to those models. Aberbach, Putnam, and Rockman (1981), for example, developed four competing "images" of the relationships, ranging from the traditional Weberian formalism to a "pure hybrid" in which the differences between politicians and senior civil servants were more nominal than real. Similarly, Nakamura and Smallwood (1980) developed five models of bureaucratic involvement in policymaking which would position patterns of interaction along much the same dimension as that defined by Aberbach, Putnam, and Rockman. My own earlier work (Peters, 1981) developed a somewhat abstract model of bureaucratic government. In addition, other work to be discussed later in this volume (see Peters, 1986a, 1986b) develops five alternative models of interaction patterns in a manner both similar to and different from those mentioned above. Then, too, Ingraham and Ban (1986) have developed a "public interest" model of the relationships of political and career appointees which attempts to

21

balance the competing interests of the two sets of actors.

Each of these sets of models offers the opportunity to compare not only the real world of one nation to the ideal world of the models but national systems to the models and then to each other. These models, then, can serve as the organizing principles for a more theoretically focused, and more truly comparative, assessment of the ways in which career civil servants and partisan politicians interact in the formulation and implementation of public policy.

Except for the problem of counting personnel and perhaps determining their social backgrounds, the research problems for comparative administration that I have outlined above may be difficult to undertake. Even if we can agree on the set of dependent variables discussed here, much work must be done before they can be used within the methodologies and approaches of the conventional social sciences. There are at least three reasons for the relatively great difficulties experienced in generating and analyzing data for the comparative study of public administration.

The first is the absence of a useful theoretical language. This is not to say that there have not been attempts to create one. Riggs and other members of the Comparative Administration Group of the American Society for Public Administration, for example, developed a huge number of neologisms in the attempt to capture differences in political systems and administrative systems. While to some extent these neologisms are useful as classificatory systems, they appear today curiously locked in time. They clearly represent the developmental concerns of the 1950s and 1960s, with nuances inadequate to capture differences among, say, the vastly different but superficially similar administrative systems of France, Spain, and Italy (see, for example, Fried, 1967; Machin, 1977). My own earlier work on the comparison of administrative systems developed its share of neologisms, especially for the relationships between interest groups and the bureaucracy, but these appear to have fallen largely on deaf ears (Peters, 1984). The language of more general organization theory also provides a series of classificatory schemes for organizations and their structural attributes but appears concerned with private sector organizations more than with public sector ones, so that many variables appear inapplicable. In many ways the language of the old and much-maligned traditional public administration (as practiced by Gulick and Urwick, Fesler, Waldo, and so on) still has a great deal to offer in the discussion of the *structure* of public administration. That language has many of the defects which Simon and others have so thoroughly analyzed, the most important being the absence of very clear connections with the behavior of individuals occupying positions in those structures, but it is still very useful in helping us begin to understand government structure.

A related problem is the shortage of indicators, even more daunting in some ways than the lack of a theoretical language. We may again usefully draw a parallel with comparative public policy. This latter field of inquiry has profitably used public expenditure data as a dependent variable, although arguably the real theoretical meaning of those data has not always been crystal clear. Data analysis has been able to precede theoretical developments or at least has preceded the development of an adequate conceptual development and justification of the major dependent variable of many or most empirical studies. If there were such a ready-made indicator, then studies might be undertaken to develop inductively a better idea of how governments are structured.

I am not advocating mindless "number crunching" but am simply observing that comparative policy studies have apparently advanced farther than comparative public administration because they went ahead and crunched some apparently meaningful numbers (Cowart, 1978; Peters, 1972; Pryor, 1968). Furthermore, substantial progress in organization theory has been made by using large bodies of data on organizations from a number of cultural settings to generate "grounded" concepts (Dunn and Swierczek, 1977; Udy, 1959).

Finally, in comparative administration minute and subtle differences appear to count a great deal. This statement resembles Pollitt's (1984) argument on behalf of social action theory as a means of approaching organizational change in the British central government. The subtle meaning attached to organizational change must be understood in context (see also Dunn and Ginzberg, forthcoming). To impose a theoretical framework in advance would therefore, according to this argument, be folly. The argument extended to its logical conclusion seems to deny the possibility of comparative analysis, but it indicates the extreme importance of contextual and highly nuanced knowledge when we attempt to interpret the characteristics of institutions such as the public bureaucracy. Comparison then becomes more difficult; indicators may become less reliable, and fewer people will have the type of detailed understanding required to make appropriate comparisons or indeed will even be able to ask the appropriate questions.

Plan of This Book

In the next four chapters I will discuss the four possible dependent variables mentioned above. I will be able only to illustrate the ways in which each of them can be used. In no case should my treatment of a given variable be regarded as exhaustive.

Chapter 2 discusses the somewhat difficult problem of defining a public employee. In it I will not only explore the question of formal and legal definitions of public employment but will also examine empirically a variety of relationships between the public and the private sector in the production of public services and discuss some of the more normative and managerial implications of shifts in production of services between the public and the private sectors.

Chapter 3 will consider the "population" of public sector organizations in the United States and the dynamics of that population, with attention to the problem of differentiating public organizations from private ones. Insofar as possible, I will try to make comparisons across political systems, but as previously noted, it may be extremely difficult to do so, given the many ways of defining *organization* in other political systems.

I will analyze behavior within public organizations by examining empirically the often used Niskanen model about the utility-maximizing behavior of public employees. As noted above, this model has been tested to some degree in the United Kingdom, but here I will compare the results obtained earlier with data from the United States—the country upon which the model is presumably based. Do American public officials appear to behave differently from their cousins across the Atlantic, and if so, why?

Finally, I will consider the power of the civil service in making public policy. This is an extremely difficult question, inasmuch as power at the upper echelons of government is generally exercised in a constrained manner. I will approach the problem by preparing a series of ideal-type models of the relationships between civil servants and their nominal political masters and will then seek to determine the extent to which the real world conforms to those ideals and what factors may explain the emergence of one form of relationship or another. Chapter 5 will in many ways be the most directly comparative of the chapters, although I have endeavored to explore the comparative dimensions of each chapter as fully as possible.

2

Public Employment
and
Public Service Industries

Fair competition between state-owned and privately owned enterprise will always end as a monopoly again. The government, as employer, must protect its own—provided there are votes involved—and cannot be trusted to act as referee.

C. Northcote Parkinson,
The Law of Delay

The first of the possible dependent variables in comparative public administration, and seemingly the easiest to cope with, is public personnel, or public employment. We are all familiar with the soldier, the fireman, the tax collector, and the public school teacher as public employees. The number of employees and the nature of public employment are difficult to determine, however, as these simple and well-known examples fail to indicate. It is increasingly difficult to say definitively who is a public employee. Furthermore, apart from merely counting heads, we must ask about the nature and caliber of people in the public service and their complex relationships with the civil society and the private economy.

This chapter will pursue two aims. First, it will discuss the use of personnel as a dependent variable—or, less formally, as a focus of inquiry—in the comparative study of public administration. I will begin with some general concerns, such as the conventional issue of being able to identify and count accurately the number of public employees, and will then address some even more difficult, and with luck interesting, questions. Second, this chapter will illustrate use of the variable to identify some dynamic features of government service provision in the late twentieth century.

Public Personnel and Comparative Administration

Organizations, even those comprising immense administrative structures, are merely large accumulations of individuals, although they may develop collective properties of their own. The first question to ask about public administration therefore relates to the constituent people: how many are they, what are they like, what do they do, and what can they do? A subsidiary question, which I will address at greater length, is whether anyone else can do the job of the public sector as well as it is done now. In this connection I will discuss a number of industries in most industrialized economies which are composed in part of public employees and in part of private sector employees. A number of complex relationships exist between the two sides of these industries. I will begin by describing the relationships between the two elements in these industries and examining the dynamics of change between them.

Many public employees are obviously public employees. Their paychecks come from government, their conditions of employment are governed by civil service laws or other public pronouncements, and they work in organizations whose names include such words as *federal* or *government* or *state*. In addition, however, public employees may be found in a number of marginal organizations in the United States, a type of organization even more prevalent in Western Europe and the Antipodes (Sharkansky, 1979).

I was recently involved in one major attempt to develop a common framework for enumerating public employees in a number of industrialized democracies (Rose et al., 1985). The data which emerged were relatively comparable, given differences in the quality of national record keeping systems and differences in definitions (see table 1), but they still suggest a number of interesting questions. Some would apply to any set of public employees, but some relate to specific categories of employment. While at first glance some of these issues may appear trivial, they are not, especially given that figures for public employment are among the bits of data that are manipulated to "prove" that government is too big, is too small, or is just the right size (the so-called Goldilocks phenomenon). The choice of one definition of public employee rather than another may make a great difference in just how large government appears, as in the case of public expenditure (Heald, 1983:12–18).

Table 1. The Scale of Public Employment

	Public employees (thousands)	Percentage of employed	Percentage of labor force	Percentage of nonagricultural workers
Britain	7,632	31.4	28.3	32.2
France	6,936	32.6	29.8	35.6
Germany	6,634	25.8	24.9	27.4
Italy	5,101	24.4	22.3	28.1
Sweden	1,553	38.2	37.4	38.8
U.S.A.	18,538	18.3	16.6	18.9

Source: Rose et al. (1985:6). Reprinted with permission of Cambridge University Press.

Far from being a trivial issue, part-time employment is extremely relevant to any discussion of the dynamics of the public sector and has been growing as a proportion of all employment in the public sector. Therefore, if we look at the total number of people who receive a paycheck from the public sector and divide that by the active work force, the public sector appears to be expanding. Rarely do we know how many of the same people are simultaneously working part time in a private sector job—frequently in the same industry. Many off-duty police officers, for example, work as private security guards. There are certainly ways of determining more accurately the amount of labor actually consumed in the public sector; we in universities are used to converting our students and our colleagues to full-time equivalents. For the naïve student of the Goldilocks phenomenon, however, part-time employment can make it appear that large changes are occurring within the public sector when perhaps little or nothing is actually happening.

The other important feature of the increase in part-time employment is that a very large proportion of the workers are women. In general, public employment is increasingly a female enterprise (Rein, 1985, 1986), especially where part-time jobs are concerned. If we count all employees equally (rather than as full-time equivalents), then public sector employment in many industrialized countries is now more than half female. The shift in employment patterns thus also reflects the changing demographics of the public sector. Given that few managerial or professional jobs are offered on a part-time basis, however, women are even more likely to be found in relatively poorly paid jobs (often without fringe benefits) in education, social welfare, and health-related occupations. The growth of female employment in the top positions in government has not been nearly as rapid as the growth in total female employment.

Another difficult problem for the enumeration of the public sector is how one counts health service employees in countries that have significant public involvement in health care. Even in Britain, where the National Health Service (NHS) is, at least in principle, a fully nationalized service, the status of some employees is far from clear. There is little question that nurses, orderlies, and other personnel employed in NHS hospitals are direct public employees, even though the NHS operates in other than financial terms at some distance from the rest of British government (Klein, 1983). When we come to the specialists (*consultants* in British parlance) who work in these same hospitals, then the case becomes slightly murky. Even though the specialists may be salaried employees of the NHS, many also have small private practices—and sometimes put their private patients into NHS hospitals (Ferriman and Wolmar, 1986). Such cases represent not part-time employment but full-time plus additional employment, and logically such specialists should be counted as full-time public employees.

Where general practitioners in the NHS are concerned, the case grows very murky indeed. A general practitioner signs a contract with the NHS that specifies the remuneration for the physician (on the basis of the number of patients on his or her panel plus other fees) and the terms of service by the physician. Is the physician a public employee, or is he or she merely a private free professional on contract to government? Is this situation really any different from government's hiring of private consultants, or garbagemen, on a contractual basis? (We counted such physicians as public employees in our comparative study.)

When health services are less directly nationalized, the status of the health professionals is even more complex. In most countries in Western Europe, for example, there is nationalized health insurance. The physicians (usually as a national organization) make a contract with a public or quasi-public organization to provide services for a certain period of time for a certain set fee schedule or perhaps for an annual salary (Carder and Klingeberg, 1980; Stone, 1980). Again, the deceptively simple question is whether these are public employees or individuals of *frei Beruf* who have entered into a contract with government. The norms of medical practice, most especially clinical freedom, militate against the bureaucratization of medical practice and excessive governmental interference, while in medical care financial considerations demand organizations that are public or quasi-public. When the organizations are quasi-public (for example, the Krankenkasse in West Germany), of course, the relationship between government and the physician is even more tenuous. Furthermore, in the United States, one can question the degree to which physicians who earn a significant portion, and sometimes 100 percent, of their income from Medicare and Medicaid patients are truly self-employed even if that portion is earned on a fee-for-service basis.

In general, education poses relatively fewer problems, but a few are still important. The British university system, to take one important example, derives approximately 85 percent of its funds from government. That money, however, is "laundered" through the University Grants Committee, composed largely of members of the universities themselves. The convenient fiction is maintained that somehow these are independent academic institutions. This fiction has been almost totally eroded by the Thatcher government's more direct involvement in university affairs—for example in advancing a proposal that tenure rights be limited and that the manner in which money is allocated to universities change—but it still remains convenient. In the United States, similar issues arise

30

in universities (such as my own) which are "tax assisted" (shouldn't we say "expenditure assisted"?) but which are not directly controlled by the state department of education or by a state board of regents and are organized and managed much as a private university would be. (Am I a civil servant?)

Another issue arises when we consider the relationship of employees of nationalized industries to government. Governments have two contradictory incentives for organizing nationalized industries. One is to set the industry apart from government so that it can operate more like an industry and respond to market forces. On the other hand, governments frequently want to be able to control these industries more than they can when the industries are distinctly separate entities (Feigenbaum, 1985; Vernon, 1984). Governments at times nationalize industries by bringing them directly into government departments; defense plants in many countries are one example. More commonly, however, governments have formed some sort of corporate structure to insulate the "firm" from direct political interference in its management decisions. The Morrisonian public corporation in Britain is a nationalized industry managed at some distance from government; the National Coal Board rather than the government controls the industry. This arrangement is extremely convenient if government does not want to seem directly involved in managerial decisions, such as whether to fight a strike vigorously. Again, the Thatcher government in Britain has strained the credibility of this separation. On the one hand it placed the apparent decision for fighting the 1984–1985 miners' strike in the hands of the National Coal Board. On the other hand it made police and other resources available so that the strike could be successfully broken. There appears to be little difficulty in arguing that the employees of these enterprises are public employees.

Again, however, the organizational ingenuity of governments has only just begun to be used in the development of public corporations. A variety of other mechanisms for corporate ownership and involvement in industry have emerged. These in turn strain our ingenuity when we try to determine who should be viewed as a public employee. Consider the case of firms which are nationalized or partially nationalized through state joint-stock corporations, such as the National Enterprise Board in the United Kingdom or Statsföretags AB in Sweden, or IRI and ENI in Italy (Redwood, 1984; Waara, 1980). These organizations are in the business of supplying capital to firms in exchange for complete or partial ownership. The notion of complete ownership may not present any difficulties for our analysis, but partial ownership certainly does. Is a person who works for a firm with 20 percent ownership by government (especially when the government's injection of capital may have been crucial in preventing bankruptcy) really a public employee? Suppose the government has 51 percent ownership or 80 percent ownership? In this case, unlike that of part-time employment, there does not seem to be any convenient mechanism for weighting the involvement of the workers.

Similarly, nationalized industries may themselves develop wholly-owned subsidiaries or may even purchase stock in private sector firms in allied industries. The annual report of the National Coal Board in Britain, for example, shows its involvement with firms interested in things such as coal gasification. Those subsidiaries appear very much to be private firms, despite the indirect involvement of government and their possible dependence on government for their very existence.

Central governments are not alone in playing this game of creating "hidden" public corporations. In Belgium, for example, groups of communes may contract with each other and may organize a quasi-private *intercommunale* in order to provide services which they would find it difficult to provide on their own, including in some instances such basics as fire protection and water (Hautphenne, 1966). Many *lan* and *kommun* governments in Sweden have assigned water, recreation, and even some social services to seemingly private corporations *(kommunägda företagens)*, whose employees do not appear in the official enumeration of public employees in Sweden.

Finally, a number of quasi-governmental corporations have been established that quite explicitly bridge the gap between the public and the private sector. To Americans the most familiar examples would be AMTRAK and Conrail, which involve the federal government in the railroad industry without doing anything so improper and socialist as to nationalize them. The Reagan administration has, however, reduced even that limited commitment to nationalization by introducing the notion of selling off Conrail to the private sector. Furthermore, the president may not wish to be viewed as responsible for the punctuality of AMTRAK trains. As in so many of my other examples, however, the organizational ploy has not altered the fact that most of the financial strings still stretch back to government. Our problem, however, is not so much financial, for if we were concerned only about the financial support of firms, the apparent size of the public sector would be quite a bit larger still (see below).

Still another major question is whether the employment generated by job training, youth employment schemes, and so on is public employment. In the Comprehensive Employment and Training Act in the United States, for example, the plan was to subsidize private firms to provide jobs for potential workers who might not otherwise be able to find a job and then to train these workers so that they could remain employed in the private sector. In reality, the program did not work quite as it had been intended, and many of the jobs created were in the public sector (more than 40 percent at the time the Reagan administration began to reduce expenditures for this program). Most industrialized countries now have similar programs, especially for youth. Should these individuals be counted as public employees, since their jobs would probably not exist if it were not for government money? Or are these programs really better treated as a thinly disguised social welfare benefit? This is an important question when we try to enumerate public sector employment in some countries. In Sweden, for example, because of the active labor market policy (Lindbeck, 1974) at some times as much as one-half to 1 percent of the total labor force may be involved in a job training program.

The preceding brief discussion should demonstrate that the problems involved in determining the size of public sector employment are far from simple to solve. An exercise conducted by the Organization for Economic Co-operation and Development at about the same time as the exercise conducted by the

University of Strathclyde in which I was involved produced figures different from ours for the same countries. In most instances the two figures had roughly the same order of magnitude, but there were some differences of as much as 43 percent (Martin, 1982; Rose et al., 1985). The consumers of such numbers, and their producers, should be extremely wary of any tabulation for which total, incontrovertible accuracy is claimed. The danger of inaccuracy and misrepresentation applies especially when numbers are used to "prove" political dogma.

A second personnel issue of great importance is the identity of the public employees. The study of "representative bureaucracy" has a long and honorable history in the study of public bureaucracies (Gboyega, 1984; Kingsley, 1944; Meier, 1975; Putnam, 1976). In general, this literature has focused on the social background—parental social class, education, race, language, gender, and so on—of civil servants. The vast majority of authors have concentrated on the recruitment for the senior, "decisionmaking" posts in the civil service rather than on recruitment for the entire civil service. The research has tended to find that the senior posts are filled primarily by well-educated males from middle-class backgrounds and from the dominant social groupings in the society (see table 2). The majority of the scholarly literature is correct in not attributing this demographic profile entirely to overt discrimination by those making the selections for the civil service. Rather, much of the pattern is attributed to the general social patterns of most societies; for example, middle-class children are more likely to receive the type of education necessary to fill posts in the senior civil service than are working-class children. Also, until recently, relatively few women worked outside the home in other than "traditional female jobs," few of which had career ladders that might bring the women into senior management positions in government.

The social background characteristics of civil service personnel have been selected as a dependent variable in the study of public administration for three reasons. First, it is intrinsically interesting to understand the characteristics of a powerful social grouping; it involves voyeurism of a certain, sociological

Table 2. Social Class Backgrounds of Senior Civil Servants (percent)

Country and year	Social class origin				Total
	Upper	Middle	Working	Other	
Australia, 1970	—[a]	—[a]	22	—	100
Belgium, 1973	13	59	11	17	100
Canada, 1957	18.1	68.7	13.2	—	100
Denmark, 1945	38.3	48.9	4.3	8.5	100
France 1971–75	40	30	14	16	100
India, 1947–63	29.2	66.1	—	4.7	100
Italy, 1965	17.4	65.4	4.7	12.5	100
Netherlands, 1973	59	26	15	—	100
Norway, 1976	—[b]	—[b]	14	15	100
Pakistan, n.d.	22.4	76.1	1.5	—	100
Republic of Korea, 1962	13.2	70.3	6.8	—	90.3
Spain, 1967	—	96	4	—	100
Sweden, 1947	9.1	81.9	3.0	6.0	100
Switzerland, 1969	—	85	15	—	100
Turkey, 1962	29.0	61.5	1.0	8.5	100
United Kingdom, 1968	21	56	19	5	101
United States, 1959	19	44	21	16	100
West Germany, 1955	13	68	0	0	81
Zambia, 1969	5	43	23	27	98

Note: In the West German survey, 19 percent did not answer; in the Korean survey, 9.7 percent did not answer.
[a]Upper and middle classes combined = 78 percent.
[b]Upper and middle classes combined = 71 percent.
Source: Peters (1984:92).

nature. Second, this investigation may have a normative purpose, attempting to demonstrate patterns of domination by certain social groups and thereby to raise questions about desirable social change (Herrmann et al., 1983; Krislov and Rosenbloom, 1981). Such investigations would, of course, produce rather different findings if the entire civil service were used rather than only the individuals at the top. While the so-called decisionmaking posts may well be crucial to the formulation of policy, the delivery of policies through the lower echelons of the civil service may be equally important to citizens, and here the gender, language, or race of the civil servant may be most important to the citizen (Goodsell, 1981). These posts do tend to be more representative of the population as a whole, especially with regard to gender.

The third reason for studying the representativeness of the public service is the most important for our purposes: there is an assumed connection between the social backgrounds of civil servants and their behavior in government. This purpose originally motivated Kingsley (1944), who feared that a British civil service recruited almost exclusively from the middle and upper classes, the Clarendon schools, and Oxbridge would find it difficult to implement the socialist program of a Labour government in postwar Britain. If this assumption were indeed correct, then information about the social characteristics of the civil service would allow one to eliminate some of the other, more difficult and expensive research options (see chapters 4 and 5). The difficulty, however, is that there does not appear to be a strong link between social background and attitudes and behavior; Putnam (1976) calls this hypothesis "plausible but ambiguous and unsubstantiated" (p. 44). The absence of relationships between social origins and attitudes is especially pronounced when social class is considered. A senior civil servant has a middle- or upper-class occupation, and people in senior positions may readily adopt the values of the middle or upper classes. There appears to be somewhat more of a relationship when less mutable factors such as race and sex are considered. In addition, there does appear to have been some relationship between the type of education received and the performance of the government bureaucracy in certain economic development roles in European countries (Armstrong, 1973).

Research into the social origins of civil servants is thus inherently interesting and is important for understanding the degree of equality which may have been attained (or not) by important segments of society. It appears less useful for attempting to explain the attitudes or behavior of civil servants in their official roles; much of their behavior appears related to their later education, training, and job socialization. Increasingly, the professional education of the civil servant is an important element in explaining behavior in the job, with perhaps the two most important professions (at least in the United States) being those of economists and lawyers (Gormley, 1983).

I should note here that the characteristics of the personnel in the senior civil service are important to consider in the study of comparative administration to the extent that these individuals constitute an identifiable "power elite" within government and society (Dogan, 1975). I will make several related points in subsequent chapters, when I address the effects of the structure of some political systems that may allow the civil service to develop into such an elite, as in France (Birnbaum, 1977; Suleiman, 1974, 1978). A behavioral element is also involved here. The relative autonomy of such an elite will allow its members to exercise governance in a manner not allowed civil servants in other political systems more bounded by values and mechanisms that require greater political accountability. Furthermore, as I will note in chapter 5, the more these senior civil servants resemble the political elites with whom they work, the more likely these two groups are to coalesce in a "village life" style of governance.

Another way of determining who civil servants are is by looking not at their social background but at their economic conditions once they are in office. In other words, how does the civil service pay compare with that being offered in the private sector, and what does any difference indicate about the power and status of the civil service? Many societies, perhaps especially the United States, have a negative image of the motivation and abilities of their civil servants, and that negative image may be reflected in the manner in which they are treated economically. Pay is one concrete means of determining whether the civil service is indeed an elite group or merely a necessary evil.

There are substantial variations in the rates of pay (see table 3), and the differences might be even greater if reliable information could be obtained on the perquisites of public employment (and private employment). What, for example, is the value of an inflation-proofed pension, which is usually only

Table 3. Ratio of Central Government Wages to per Capita Income

Nation	Ratio
High	
Burundi	15.11
Senegal	9.90
Cameroon	7.39
Egypt	5.70
India	4.80
Low	
Austria	1.06
Australia	1.16
Singapore	1.16
Norway	1.48
Sweden	1.49

Source: Heller and Tait (1983).

available to public employees? In many developing countries civil servants average many times the per capita income in the economy, reflecting in part the central role which the state tends to play in those societies and the absorption of a very large share of the educated and trained manpower into the public sector (Heller and Tait, 1983). On the other hand, in most industrialized countries the average civil servant earns about the same amount as the average person in the economy. In fact, many industrialized countries have made explicit efforts to keep public pay scales very closely aligned with private sector pay.

The issue of pay comparability is more than merely an exercise in accounting, however; it is a political and managerial exercise as well (Bargas, 1983; Duffau, 1983). Politically, civil service pay is a symbol to many people. They believe, usually wrongly, that the civil service is overpaid and underworked and that its pay should be reduced. Certainly the Reagan and Thatcher governments coming into office have believed that many people have sought to alter that situation (Peters, 1986b).

Depending upon the study (and the author), civil servants in the United States are 20+ percent behind their private sector counterparts, and those in the United Kingdom are approximately 15 percent behind (Advisory Commission on Federal Pay, 1985; Council of Civil Service Unions, 1986). Furthermore, control over civil service pay can be a means of managing a thinly disguised incomes policy, especially if, as in the United Kingdom, the public sector employs a significant proportion of the total work force. Private sector employers, also knowing that a major competitor for employees is keeping their wage increases low, can do so themselves so that there can be some general impact on wages and eventually perhaps on prices.

The question of the attraction and retention of employees, mentioned above with respect to private sector employees, is the major managerial issue with respect to civil service pay. Even if, as in the United States, total public employment remains at about the same level, relative to total employment, the decisions made by the public employees appear increasingly important for the society. Therefore we should—to paraphrase a former president—try to hire only the best. The political need to suppress wages thus conflicts with the managerial need to hire talented people in a competitive job market. This statement is especially true in managerial and professional positions. In the United States, if pay for the entire civil service is some 20 percent below that for comparable workers in the private sector, then that of senior management is at least 40 or 50 percent below. This gap and several other factors have contributed to a very high rate of attrition among the Senior Executive Service. The fundamental point is that the negative image of the civil servant may be a self-fulfilling prophecy: if we think poorly of the abilities of the average civil servant and pay him or her accordingly, then the public service will be able to attract only employees of poor quality.

As we have seen, any number of additional questions could be asked about public personnel—career patterns, personnel management, and so on. Still, the three discussed briefly here are central. In addition, these questions appear central to the

development of a conception of comparative public administration which would bring it more closely in line with other
aspects of comparative politics, most especially comparative
public policy. Having cleared away some of the more general
underbrush, we can proceed to another important and not unrelated question.

Public and Private Employment

Much of the conventional discussion of relationships between state and society has assumed that there was a clear
distinction between the two sets of actors. In Anglo-Saxon
countries, at least, the state has been perceived as the more
limited of the two actors, with its powers prescribed by legal or
constitutional provisions and its expenditures and employees
clearly identified through budgets and organization charts
(Dyson, 1980). The functions of government were assumed to
be the tasks which government has been given a clear legal, or
even constitutional, authorization to perform.

As I have already noted and will show at even greater length
in chapter 3, the clear analytic separation between state and
society no longer exists. A number of forces—for example, the
development of greater corporatist tendencies in most industrialized countries (Schmitter and Lehmbruch, 1982), pressures on government to restrict its expenditures (Tarschys,
1985), and demands for improved policy performance (Salamon, 1981a; Savas, 1979)—have combined to produce a
greater blending of state and society. This blending is usually
discussed in terms of the encroachment of government on the
private sector, but more recently the private sector appears to
be making incursions into areas which have been strictly governmental. This analysis will be concerned with possible relationships between the public and private sectors in terms of
employment and the relative share of public and private employment in different "industries."

Government is involved in a number of industries—in all of
them if we count the regulatory impact of government. Some

of these industries we regard as peculiarly public (defense and police protection), while in others we consider government to have a relatively minor role (banking). There are virtually no monopolies, even in employment terms, however, and most industries have some public as well as some private employment (Ginzberg, 1976). Furthermore, as we will demonstrate, despite the discussion of government's emergence as a dominant force in modern society, it appears that the private sector has assumed a larger share (in employment terms) of industries which we have typically considered public sector monopolies.

Some limited data (most of it from the United States) are available to illustrate the relationships between public and private employment. I will begin by using a rather formal definition of employment and will leave aside some of the possibilities of coproduction between citizen and the government (Gershuny, 1978; Rose, 1985b). That is, I will not consider involvement in neighborhood watch for crime prevention as employment, although it is a productive activity and probably does add to neighborhood safety just as the hiring of a private guard would. I do not deny the importance of these activities, but here we are concerned with the generation of formal employment, through either the public sector or the market.

I have already noted that, when the person on the street thinks of a public employee, he or she is likely to think of the civil servant, the policeman, the soldier, or someone comparable. These are all clearly public employees, but the employment relationship between government and its citizens may extend beyond those who simply receive a paycheck directly from government (Blumenthal, 1979). Furthermore the relationships may be even more complex than became evident in the definitional questions I raised above. In addition to people who are direct employees of government, we can think of four "mixed" models of public employment. These are four variations on the theme that few functions in society are now the exclusive domain either of government or of the private sector and that, in fact, most goods and services are generated by the interaction of the two sectors. These four models include the types of relationships between the public and the private sector that are included in van der Wielen's (1983) concept of the "semipublic sector" as well as some more complex relationships which were not discussed in her more economic analysis of employment in the Netherlands.

Table 4. Department of Defense Prime Contracts as a Percentage of Total Sales, 1985

Contractor	Percentage
McDonald—Douglas	91.7
General Dynamics	91.1
Grumman	89.6
Lockheed	62.4
Martin Marietta	61.6
Rockwell	55.6

Sources: U.S. Department of Defense (1985); Standard and Poor (1985).

The first interactive relationship, which is perhaps the most familiar, can be termed *contractual*. Government frequently contracts with firms in the private sector to buy goods and services and thereby generates employment in the private sector. This relationship has been discussed most frequently in defense industries, where government is frequently the monopsonistic purchaser for certain products and virtually the sole customer for some large firms such as McDonald-Douglas, General Dynamics, and Grumman (see table 4). It should be remembered, however, that this monopsonistic relationship is not confined to defense; a large number of consulting firms exist for the sole purpose of advising government on social policy, health policy, housing policy, and other types of policy. In addition to the military industrial complex, there is a social policy-consulting complex as well, referred to in Washington as the beltway bandits.

Even if government is not a monopsonistic purchaser of a product, its purchases will still generate significant employment. As table 5 shows, military expenditures in 1981 accounted for only 29 percent of the jobs created by government purchases from the private sector; state and local governments accounted for more than half of all employment generated. These purchases could be anything from complex computer systems to school buses to paper clips. Furthermore, the military share in the "contract state" is now lower than it was in

Table 5. Private Employment Created by Contractual Relationships with Government in the United States

	Total as percentage of labor force	Distribution		
		Defense	Other federal	State and local
1964	8.7	30.6	11.3	58.1
1970	9.5	25.3	9.3	65.4
1975	8.8	25.0	14.5	60.5
1980	7.8	28.9	17.1	54.0
1981	7.6	29.0	17.1	53.9

Source: Employment and Training Administration (annual).

the early 1960s, although not as low as it was during the 1970s. On the other hand, however, the contract share has been increasing as a percentage of total defense employment and to some degree reflects the substitution of capital for manpower in defense.

Contracting is not, however, a peculiarly American phenomenon. All governments, save perhaps those in fully state-owned economies, make purchases from the private sector. In Britain, for example, it is estimated that some 225,000 jobs are created directly, and another 170,000 indirectly, by military purchases by government; another 120,000 jobs are created by overseas sales of defense equipment (Cmnd. 9763-II, 1986). While this figure is not as large as in the United States, the total is still some 3 percent of total private employment and almost 10 percent of manufacturing employment (see also De-Grasse, 1983). Likewise, some large British firms (Marconi, some shipyards, and so forth) are as dependent as General Dynamics upon defense business. Also, while until recently governments in Europe supplied their own policy advice through the civil service, there has been some growth in private consulting firms, many of them American management consultants, that contract to provide such services as well.

The second direct employment relationship between the public and private sectors is labeled *complementary*. In this relationship government and the private sector may be providing similar services or exactly the same service. Examples of this type of relationship would include private police services, private education, and the various courier services that have begun to compete with the U.S. Postal Service for certain types of deliveries. The reasons for the development of these complementary services are rather varied. In some instances, it is believed that a superior product—either education or mail delivery—can be created by the private sector. In others, a concentration of service can be supplied in a particular geographical area which would otherwise be covered only periodically; for example, private police hired to patrol continuously a neighborhood which otherwise would be covered only on regular patrols. Or the private sector may be able to deliver the service in a particular manner—for example, religious instruction in school—which could not be obtained or allowed in the public sector. Complementary provision may also be a management device for government, so that in the case of labor disputes or other difficulties some services may still be provided. Finally, as many local governments face budgetary constraints and are increasingly unable to provide certain types of services, some private provision may supplement public provision to retain the same volume of service.

The latter example brings us to the problem of attempting to distinguish, in some instances, contractual services from complementary services. The privatization of a number of public services (for example, garbage collection) could be regarded as a contract for the provision of a service or as a case in which the private sector provides a complementary service for government. In this analysis we will include the privatization of services as examples of complementary functions. We do this

44

because, unlike the case in which weapons are purchased from a defense contractor, the same type of good or service is being created rather than an intermediate product for the creation of the service (such as defense) that is purchased from the private sector. The two could also be differentiated on the basis of whether the public sector continued to provide some services after the inception of the private provision, but such differentiation would require greater knowledge of each program than is practical for this study, inasmuch as it is being conducted at quite a high level of aggregation.

If we wished to refine our analysis even further, we might differentiate between components of an industry which are purely complementary and those which are more competitive. A purely complementary service would be one which provides a service that government is not really trying to provide. Night watchmen, for example, have almost never been public employees, although they fulfill a type of policing function and are a component of the same protection "industry" as the public police. Parcel delivery would appear to be a competitive service, with both the U.S. Postal Service and its competitors advertising vigorously for business. If one gains a larger market share, the other will almost inevitably lose.

The third mixed model of public/private employment relationships is less commonly discussed. This I have termed an *adversarial* relationship, in which government action generates employment in the private sector designed to protect private sector clients from the activities of government. This type of relationship has existed for years, of course. Defense attorneys in the legal system are a prime example, but there appears to have been a rapid growth of other types of adversarial occupations. The public perception of an increasing tax burden, for example, and the increasing complexity in the tax law, have produced a huge increase in the numbers of tax advisers, accountants, and, for the less affluent, storefront advisers (H. & R. Block and so on). The need for such services is unlikely to vanish with the implementation of tax reform. Likewise, in universities and large firms, the need to comply with state and federal equal opportunity laws has created the occupation of "affirmative action officer," and the threat of inspection by the Occupational Safety and Health Administration has generated a safety industry which tells its clients how to comply with (or how to avoid) regulations. While these occupations exist entirely within the private sector (except perhaps at state universities), and exist in opposition to government, in all likelihood they would not exist *without* government. Furthermore, as government increases in perceived magnitude and importance for industry and for individuals, these adversarial occupations appear likely to continue increasing in the numbers of people they employ.

The fourth type of relationship between public sector activity and employment in the private sector may be termed *transfer*. In this relationship the public sector either transfers resources to individuals in the private sector to be used for certain specified purposes or gives transfers to the providers of services. In this instance I am speaking not of fungible transfers such as Social Security payments but rather of transfers that can be used only for a specific purpose. The most obvious example is in medicine, where significant employment has arguably been generated as a result of the greater availability of public medical insurance or direct payments for groups that might otherwise have been excluded from the medical marketplace. Furthermore, additional services and providers have entered the market; for example, additional extended care facilities for the elderly have opened under Medicare. Food stamps have almost certainly helped to create additional demands for food, and greater agricultural employment, although the plight of the American farmer in the 1980s might seem to belie this statement.

The transfer relationship poses a problem for our purposes in that it is more difficult to ascribe employment directly to transfers than to government purchases. If a physician is earning 50 percent or more of his or her income from public medical programs, should that physician be counted as a public employee, and should we assume that the employment would

46

not have existed without the public program? Models estimating the employment generated by the contract state have been developed (Stern, 1975), but I am not aware of existing models for estimating employment generated by the transfer state. As a result, some of my attempts to measure such employment will be rather crude, especially in the case of health and social services. In particular, such models might involve counterfactual elements. Would the elderly or the poor have consumed the same amount of medical services if the public programs had not been available?

In short, government generates employment in a number of ways. One is by hiring people directly. The other four involve a less direct relationship between the public sector and the employee, but the relationship exists nonetheless. These additional forms of employment generation confound attempts to measure the "size" of the public sector and may make the Goldilocks phenomenon even more of a fairy tale. Perhaps more important, these forms of employment generation may confound the efforts of people in and out of government who want to impose more control and greater accountability in the public sector. It is especially difficult to enforce accountability when the people responsible for the actual success or failure of a program may be beyond the direct control of the people who are being held accountable politically (Hague and Smith, 1971).

Two particular recent examples in the United States make this point rather well. One is the well-known case of the overcharging and apparent fraud by General Dynamics as well as by a number of other defense contractors. These incidents were deemed to be scandals *within the federal government* almost as much as for the individuals who had committed the illegal acts. While it is certainly true that the Pentagon is responsible for monitoring compliance with contracts and preventing fraud, as far as has been reported there have been no real illegalities committed by public employees. Similarly, overbilling by doctors on Medicaid and Medicare is often cited as an example of the general failings of social programs; again, not the programs per se but the private providers are at fault. Regardless of the direct activities of its employees, government will apparently be held accountable for the failings of its indirect employees as well.

Declining Monopolies

With the idea of the five types of possible employment relationships between government and the private sector in mind (direct employment plus four types of indirect employment), we can begin to consider some evidence about the employment of individuals in a number of functional areas. The evidence for indirect employment in some of these functional areas is rather weak, especially across time, but even these available data indicate that government does not have any real monopolies of employment. Indeed government may be a minority provider of employment in policy areas which have been central to the definition of government in the past (Rose, 1976), for example defense.

Table 6 presents data for public and private employment in twelve policy areas. The functional areas are listed in declining degree of "publicness" of their employment and are labeled according to whether they are contractual, complementary, or adversarial. I was not able to obtain adequate information on employment generated by transfers, although I will later refer to employment generated in this manner and will mention some very rough estimates. Of these policy areas, which include some of the traditional areas assumed to be solely government (defense and police protection), education is the most public function, but it is only 85 percent public. This policy area would, however, have been even less public if I had been able to disaggregate the effects of only educational purchases from the total of state and local government purchases shown in table 5. As education is the largest single expenditure for state and local government, it is almost certain to be a significant amount of the private sector employment generated. Education accounts for approximately 35 percent of total state and

Table 6. Public and Private Employees in Functional Areas, 1980

Functional area	Public employees (thousands)	Private employees (thousands)	Percentage of public employees
Education	6,959	1,231	85.0
Post Office	664	250[a]	72.6
Highways	564	261[b]	68.4
Tax Administration	426	280[c]	60.3
Police	672	450[d]	59.9
Defense	3,021	2,100[e]	59.0
Social Services	622	1,160[f]	34.5
Transportation	752	2,010	30.9
Health	1,674	3,987	29.6
Gas/electricity/water	314	821	26.8
Banking	21	1,629	1.2
Telecommunications	8	1,376	0.5

[a]Private express services, couriers, etc.
[b]Contracting firms involved in highway construction.
[c]Estimate of tax accountants and staff, H. & R. Block employees, and so forth, including seasonal employees.
[d]Industry estimate of number of private guards, private policemen, and so forth.
[e]U.S. Department of Labor estimate of employment generated by military purchases.
[f]Private social work and philanthropy; large percentage employed only part time (volunteers excluded).
Sources: U.S. Bureau of the Census (1969; 1974; 1982); U.S. Department of Defense (annual); Office of Personnel Management (biennial); Employment and Training Administration (annual).

local expenditure. If we assume that education had the same employment generation effects as other types of expenditures, then educational purchases would have accounted for an additional 1.6 million employees in the private sector in 1980. Given that a great deal of educational expenditure is direct salaries and wages of teachers and other workers (approximately

64 percent, as compared with only about 25 percent for the rest of state and local government), 1.6 million is probably an over-estimate; we can be sure, however, that the figure would be large.

Both police and defense—perhaps the two most distinctive functions of government—are slightly less than 60 percent public, although their relationship with the private sector is quite different. Most police employment in the private sector is complementary, while for defense the relation is clearly con-tractual. Even tax collection, certainly a function over which government could be assumed to have a monopoly (but re-member tax farming), has generated a huge number of private sector employees dedicated to making the collection of taxes more difficult (or less profitable) for government. Total employ-ment in the tax industry is only 60 percent in the public sector.

Table 7. Changes in Public and Private Employment, 1970–1980

| | Percentage of public employees | |
Policy area	1970	1980
Education	87	85
Post office	92	73
Highways	74	68
Tax administration	90[a]	60
Police	85	60
Defense	63	59
Social services	26	35
Transportation	33	31
Health	26	30
Gas/electricity/water	25	27
Banking	1	1
Telecommunications	—[b]	1

Note: For definitions of types of employment, see table 6.
[a]Very rough estimate.
[b]Less than 0.5 percent.
Sources: See table 6; Peters (1985b).

The distribution of public and private employment in these "industries" has not been stable over time. The movements in the shares of employment have been almost entirely in the direction of creating a fifty-fifty state in which the public and private sectors tend to have relatively equal shares of employment in each policy area. As table 7 shows, policy areas with higher levels of public employment in 1970 tended to become more private in the decade leading up to 1980, while those which were more private tended to become more public. The shifts were especially noticeable in the post office, where the development of a number of courier services severely reduced the government monopoly in the delivery of parcels and information. The trend has, if anything, been accelerating since 1980 with the increase in technological capabilities for transmitting information electronically.

There has also been a very large movement toward private policies because of increasing crime rates and local budgets which have not kept pace with the demands being placed upon them. In addition, ideological and efficiency criteria have led to the privatizing of some jails and other correctional facilities and hence a larger private sector involvement in this policy area. This area has of course traditionally been a monopoly of government, and the growth of so much private policing raises a number of questions about the legitimate use of force in society, given that relatively few states have developed statutes that adequately define the duties and responsibilities of, and the limits on, private police personnel.

The increasing public role in employment in the policy areas with lower government employment—the social services, health, and local utilities—is not as dramatic as the relative decline in public employment in other areas, but it is still important. Just as government appears to be losing its monopoly over its traditional activities in the United States, the private sector is losing its monopoly or virtual monopoly on social service functions. This statement is, of course, not news to those who have been concerned about the increased social responsibilities of government, especially the federal government. Although the evidence is not as complete as that actually presented in the tables, even the cutbacks made during the Reagan administration have apparently not appreciably affected the growth of *total* employment in these policy areas. Rather, there has been a shift from federal employment (still not as great as it is often imagined to be) into employment in state and local governments. It is most interesting, however, that the shift in the direction of public involvement in these areas is not as rapid as the shift in the direction of the private sector for mail delivery and police protection.

The decline in the monopoly position of the private sector in the social services would be more dramatic, however, if the effects of regulation on these sectors were included. It would be more dramatic still if the impact of transfers, our fourth category of indirect employment relationships, and of social insurance were considered. As noted, it is questionable that a physician who receives the majority of his or her income from Medicare and Medicaid patients is really self-employed. Thus if we assume that the 28 percent of all personal medical expenses which are covered by Medicare and Medicaid were translated into an equal level of employment, then health care in 1980 would actually have been more than half public, as compared with the figure of approximately 40 percent public in 1970, derived using the same method of calculation. The impact of funding in the social services would not have been as great, although programs such as Title XX of the Social Security Amendments have provided significant levels of funding for day care and other social service programs whose employees were considered to be private sector employees. Thus, although I would not be willing to go quite as far as Ginzberg (1976) and argue that one job in three in the United States is actually a product of government activity, the figures normally reported for public sector employment do appear to understate seriously the levels of employment generated by government. On the other hand, however, many of our traditional conceptions of government activity are being eroded by the increasing involvement of the private sector.

Some Limited Comparisons

Unfortunately, we have not as yet been able to develop comparative examples with these types of data that are as extensive as we might have liked. The reason is in part that some of the evidence, especially about the complementary services, involves estimates by those involved in the service area as well as by the U.S. Department of Labor. With a few heroic assumptions, based largely on census data, as well as some detailed analysis by some economists, I have been able to make some limited comparisons with both Canada and Sweden.

The data for Canada are based upon two sources. The first is the application of a standard input-output model of the economy (Bucovetsky, 1979) and includes only the effects of government purchases but not the type of complementary services discussed earlier for the United States. The indirect employment effects were calculated for only six categories (see table 8). Of these, health and education were the most public, with more than 80 percent of the employment being direct public employment.

Table 8. Direct Public Employment and Other Forms of Employment Relationships, Canada, 1971 (percent)

	Direct	Indirect[a]	Complementary
Defense	76.5	23.5	—
Education	81.8	9.0	9.2
Health	85.4	8.9	5.7
Police	79.9	—	20.1
Social welfare	67.1	—	32.9
Other municipal	75.0	25.0	N/A
Other provincial	62.4	37.6	N/A
Other federal	73.9	26.1	N/A
Total	80.3	19.7	N/A

Note: N/A = not available.
[a]Employment generated by government purchases of goods and services.
Sources: Bucovetsky (1979); Foot (1979); Census of Canada, 1971 (1971, sec. 3).

Defense employment is much more of a direct government employment "industry" in Canada than in the United States. The same may well be true of most other nations that tend to purchase a large proportion of their military hardware from the United States or from other arms-exporting countries. Therefore, if we consider that additional purchases made by allied countries from American arms suppliers contribute to the overall defense of the United States, then the actual indirect employment generated by defense in the United States, as reported in table 6, would be greater. Any attempt to determine just how much greater, however, would resemble an exercise in metaphysics.

The second source of data for Canada was the Census of Occupations, which gave figures for people employed in complementary services such as private education and private policing. Especially in social welfare services, a service which has come to be regarded as increasingly public in Canada still has a significant private component. Also, there is a significant private policing function although one that is apparently not as significant as in the United States. In short the private sector has significant involvement in providing goods and services in Canada, although not as great as in the United States; this is true despite some feelings that the public sector is increasingly dominant. Unfortunately, we lack longitudinal data to determine whether the same movements that we have found for the United States are valid in Canada, but impressionistic evidence would seem to justify the assumption that they apply in areas such as policing and education.

We have even fewer data for Sweden, although those that we do have show some similar patterns as those found in the United States and Canada. We do not have any reliable information on the employment generated by government purchases of goods and services, although in an economy in which approximately two-thirds of gross national product passes through the public sector, the figure is likely to be sizable. Even with a government so large, and with well over one-third of the labor force employed in the public sector (Peters, 1985c), there is still substantial private sector employment. Some of this

Table 9. Public and Private Employment in Sweden, 1980 (percent)

	Public	Private
Education	96	4
Health	94	6
Social Sciences	93	7
Police	82	18

Sources: Peters (1985c); Statistiska Centralbyrån (annual, 1980).

employment is in industries generally considered to be public in Sweden.

Table 9 provides for Sweden some of the same information that was presented for Canada and the United States but only in the areas of health, education, welfare, and police. Interestingly, the highest private involvement in any of these areas was in policing. Apparently even in a country with a (relatively) low crime rate and a relatively large and centralized police force, there is still a demand for private services to supplement available public protection services. Perhaps, given the especially extensive development of the welfare state in Sweden, there was relatively little private employment in health, education, or welfare. Although the available information is not sufficiently detailed for presentation in tabular form, private provision of social services seems to have been declining over the past several decades.

Conclusion

The data we have presented, while limited in their scope and requiring more interpretation and analysis, do have some important implications for the nature of government in the last decades of the twentieth century. Most obviously, the declining separation between the public and the private sectors will affect the accountability and control of government. This is a classic question in the study of public administration but still one of great importance. In the United States the scandals of Watergate, Brilab, and Abscam elevated questions of the control of government and public officials to the front pages. Few countries have escaped similar scandals involving public officials.

A more subtle and perhaps more important struggle, however, is under way out of the headlines. Because of the existence and expansion of the "contract state" and the development of privately marketed services to complement publicly provided services, it is increasingly difficult to determine who is ultimately responsible for the provision of a service and who is merely acting in the name of government. This ambiguity presents problems for both the public official and the citizen. In the case of the public official responsible for delivering a service, the responsibility for delivery and financial probity may be distinct from the actual delivery of the service. The public official is then in the uncomfortable position of having to point elsewhere when things go wrong. This stance is frequently, if inaccurately, perceived by citizens as an indication that government is really incapable of governing effectively, and as another example of the proverbial "buck-passing" behavior of public bureaucrats.

Some of the issues facing public administrators (for example, cost overruns on defense contracts) are expensive and certainly troublesome, but some of the less frequently discussed accountability problems more greatly threaten the continuation of the system of government to which we have become accustomed. What role, for example, should private police have in the enforcement of public law? Do they have the same rights in the use of deadly force that publicly hired policemen have when they are enforcing a public law? Do the duties of the private police officer extend to the protection of the entire community while he or she is on duty or only to the protection of individuals who employ the officer? How should the public police regulate the hiring, licensing, and use of the private police which function within their jurisdictions? These are more than trivial questions of implementation, for if the private police are allowed to behave in an unregulated and un-

accountable manner, the negative image created may be difficult for the public police to escape, and the authority which
the public sector should exercise over behavior in the society
may be weakened.

For the citizen, somewhat different versions of the same
problems are created by the increased intermingling of the public and the private. Government is frequently seen by citizens
as complex and incapable of being influenced by their actions.
For those who lack a feeling of "political competence" or perhaps "administrative competence" (Almond and Verba, 1963:
136ff.), the development of a whole range of complementary
and competing services may increase the feelings of frustration
with "the system" and may make the resolution of complaints, or the answering of simple questions, even more difficult. Citizens frequently feel, although perhaps not as often as
is sometimes assumed (Goodsell, 1985), that they are being
given the runaround by government. If the complexity of service delivery continues to increase as it has in the recent past,
then that perception is likely to increase. In a capitalist and
democratic society, free choice and the availability of alter-
natives are valued. If the options become too complex, however, a little dose of simple monopoly may also be valued. The
confusion resulting from the dissolution of the AT & T monopoly over phone services may be educational for understanding
analogous problems in the public sector. Advocates of more
efficient government (Niskanen, 1971; Tullock, 1974) have frequently recommended that government monopolies be dis-
solved, but they may not have taken sufficiently into account
the confusion and potential problems of accountability associated with the creation of a quasi-market in the public sector.

The difficulties arising from the mixed provision of most
public services also present problems for scholars of government and public administration. Most of our models of administration assume a neat hierarchical arrangement between
those at the top of an organization and the field staff that actually delivers the service. Students of public administration sel-
dom place significant emphasis on contract monitoring and
bargaining with private sector providers. Perhaps the closest

we have come to doing so is in the implementation literature, which recognizes that many of the "clearance points" in the successful implementation of a program are in the private sector (Pressman and Wildavsky, 1973). Others concerned with "bottom-up" implementation (Hjern and Hull, 1982; Hjern and Porter, 1981) have argued that the best way to understand what happens in government is to understand the bargaining arrangements at the lowest level of the organizational pyramid. These insights do not, however, appear to have been translated effectively into the curricula of most schools of public administration. There appears to be a need for a reconceptualization of many aspects of public administration as a field and for greater attention to these difficult problems.

The existence of complementary and transfer relationships may also raise important questions about the efficiency of government. It has now become the conventional wisdom for some, especially on the political right, that government services are inherently inefficient (Hanusch, 1983; Niskanen, 1971; Pierce, 1981; for some empirical evidence see Ahlbrandt, 1973; Spann, 1977). Furthermore, some observers, such as Niskanen (1971), have argued that the efficiency of government services could be improved by eliminating the monopolies held by existing bureaus and by creating competition. In the real world, however, in addition to creating confusion, the development of complementary services in the public and private sectors may simply mean the duplication of physical facilities, staffs, and expenditures. Moreover, we know from a number of studies that different government services have different optimal catchment areas (Bennett, 1980:293ff.; Newton, 1978). The breaking up of a monopoly may actually mean the creation of two or more suboptimal service areas where a single optimally sized service area had previously existed. Pleas for building in competition between public and private providers should thus be accompanied by a careful analysis of the production and consumption characteristics of the service in question. Everything else being equal, for example, services requiring large capital infrastructures may be more efficiently delivered by a monopoly (be it public or private) than would a service which is more labor intensive. This reasoning is, of course, analogous to the natural monopoly arguments for the regulation of public utilities (Wolf, 1979).

In summary, most policy and program areas in modern societies have both public and private service providers. Furthermore, most policy areas are tending toward more equal levels of participation (in employment terms) of public and private providers. While these tendencies have been lauded by some as indicating the creation of an analogue to the market in public services with associated improvements in efficiency, these changes can be questioned on the grounds both of public accountability and of economic efficiency. It is consequently important for both researchers and practitioners to understand the trends and to develop an understanding of the dynamics of change.

While this chapter may have appeared to have rambled across a wide expanse of the public administration landscape, it displays several coherent themes. First, public employees are not as easy to identify as we might have thought. Any number of conceptual and operational difficulties must be addressed before we can say definitively just how large the work force employed in the public sector really is. This statement is intended as an antidote to the simplistic enumerations which have been developed largely for political purposes.

Second, even after we conduct the exercise and have every public employer identified and safely under glass, a significant amount of private sector employment remains the direct product of public sector activities. Some of that employment is generated because government buys a huge quantity of goods and services in the private market, ranging from paper clips to missiles. Some of it is generated because government does not do some things as well as it might or does not do them as some citizens would like. Private sector organizations may therefore jump in to fill the gap. Also, employment is generated to protect individuals and organizations from laws or at least to ensure compliance with those laws at the lowest cost. Given the complex relationships which exist between the public and the private sectors, it is important to remember the industries within which people work rather than thinking simply in terms of the public and the private sectors. When we do so, we can better understand the complexity of the evolving world of public administration and can develop concepts and ideas that will be of greater utility to both practitioners and scholars.

3

Organizations as the Building Blocks of Government

(with Brian W. Hogwood)

Public and Private are not categories of nature; they are categories of history, culture and law.

Dwight Waldo

Public administration, which as we have seen is a collection of individuals, is also a collection of organizations. Indeed, government itself is little more than a collection of a large number of organizations. Even those actors who might be thought to engage in more personalistic forms of government decision-making, such as prime ministers, have begun to build extensive organizations around themselves. Although few chief executives and legislatures have staffs as large as those available to their counterparts in the United States, staff size has been increasing almost everywhere (Campbell, 1983). To study government is therefore to a great extent to study organizations. It is, however, deceptively easy to say that we must study organizations in government; a number of conceptual and methodological issues associated with the study of government organizations make such research difficult.

Some of these difficulties in studying public organizations were mentioned in the first chapter. In this chapter we will elaborate on some of the points made earlier and will then proceed to address one research problem on government organizations in the United States. This chapter will also present some more limited material from several other countries to illuminate the findings for the United States. If nothing else, this chapter demonstrates the usefulness of organizations as a unit of analysis when studying government, especially in the United States, where the definition of public organizations is much clearer than in many other industrialized countries. Organizations do appear, however, to have some more general utility for comparative analysis as well.

The Study of Government Organizations

If we are to use government organizations as a basic building block in our analysis of government, it would be helpful to be able to identify the organizations. The task is not as easy as it might appear. Even within a single country, the variety of organizational forms and the variety of internal structuring of large organizations (Seidman and Gilmour, 1986) make it difficult to determine just what a public organization is. Furthermore, as we saw in chapter 2, it is increasingly difficult for students of government to determine who public personnel and their organizations are. While it may be fruitless to try to draw a strict line between the public and the private sector, it is still crucial to be able to place some organizations within, and some others beyond, the universe which we intend to study. The definitional problems associated with the study of public organization, therefore, can be disaggregated into two component problems: what is a public *organization?* and what is a *public* organization?

Organizations, and formal organizations, have been defined in any number of ways. Blau and Scott (1962), for example, concentrate on networks of social relations and shared orientations in structures that have been deliberately established for a certain purpose. Katz and Kahn (1978) take a full five pages to define an organization. Their open-systems approach emphasizes recurrent patterns of activity, the maintenance of a boundary between the organization and its environment, and the importation of energy and resources from the organizational environment. Simon, Smithburg, and Thompson (1950) refer to a "planned system of cooperative effort" (p. 5). Many

Figure 1. Structure of the U.S. Department of Agriculture.

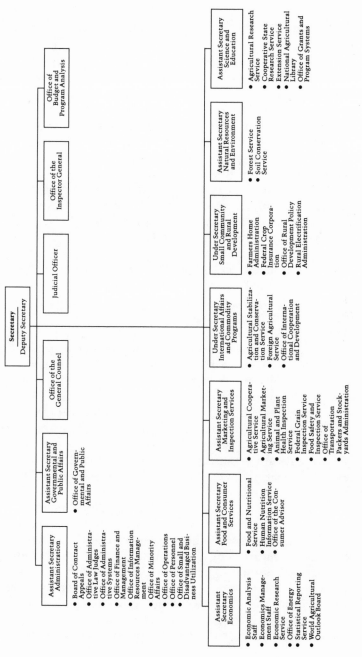

Source: Office of the Federal Register (1984:816).

books discussing public administration and public organizations never even bother to try to define an organization.

Many of the definitions offered for formal organizations present difficulties when we study organizations in government. With the Blau and Scott definition, for example, one might find that, in many nominal organizations, for example an agency in the U.S. federal government, there may *not* be shared orientations among the career civil servants and the political executives brought in from the outside to supervise them. Such appears to have been particularly the case during the Nixon and Reagan administrations, when many civil servants did not share the antigovernment biases of many political appointees (Aberbach and Rockman, 1976; Peters, 1986a). Furthermore, many nominally public organizations perform tasks different from, or supplementary to, those mentioned in the legislation which established them. Are these any less formal organizations, or are they merely different manifestations of common problems of collective action?

Many of the same criticisms could be applied to the other definitions of formal organizations, but this chapter is not intended as an exercise in definitional analysis or semantics. Rather, we can consider specific examples of public organizations and identify similar definitional difficulties. Figures 1 and 2 are the organization charts of two cabinet departments in the U.S. federal government, taken directly from the *United States Government Manual*. While it is clear that both of these departments are organizations by almost any definition, it is less clear what, if anything, we should consider a formal organization at the subdepartmental level.

The case of the components of the U.S. Department of Agriculture is certainly clearer than the case of the components in the Department of Housing and Urban Development (HUD). Within the Department of Agriculture, there are a number of well-defined agencies, for example, the Forest Service, the Farmers Home Administration, and the Animal and Plant Health Inspection Service. In addition, almost all of these bodies have a basis in public law, and so we can find out when they came into being and what their nominal powers are. So far

Figure 2. Structure of the U.S. Department of Housing and Urban Development.

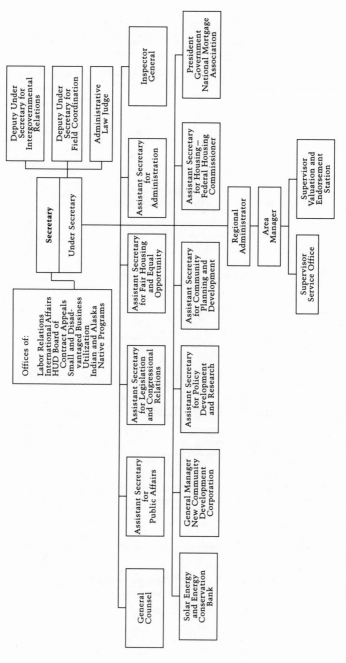

Source: Office of the Federal Register (1984:825).

Figure 3. Program Structure under the U.S.
Department of Housing and Urban Development.

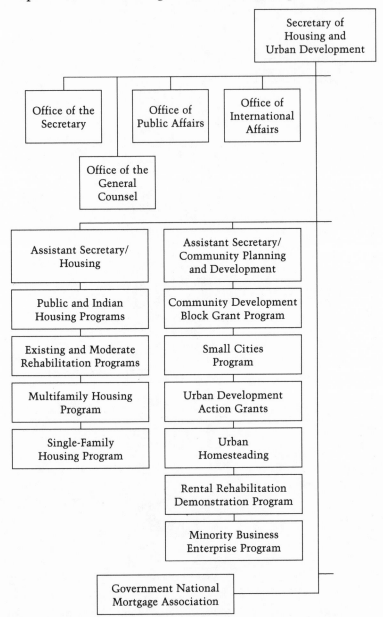

Source: U.S. Department of Housing and Urban Development, *Annual Report* (1984).

Organizations as Building Blocks

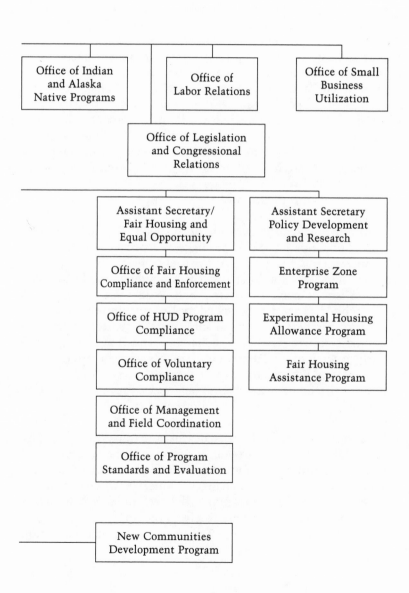

so good, but below the level of the agencies which we can see on this chart, we encounter things such as "programs" which also may have some structural manifestations. Someone will be in charge of these programs, and there will be a hierarchy—sometimes an extensive hierarchy—responsible for their administration. As important as programs are in government (Rose, 1985a), are they organizations? The question may appear unimportant, but it certainly is not if researchers (such as ourselves) are interested in organizations as a unit of analysis in government and are concerned to recognize changes in the number and type of organizations. One need not go so far as the scholars in organization theory who have been attempting to develop a cladistic pattern of identification for organizations analogous to the system that might be developed for organisms in biology (Aldrich, 1979; McKelvey, 1982; McKelvey and Aldrich, 1983). Even more modest theoretical efforts, however, will require specification of the domain to which the theory extends.

To some degree the question of the level at which one looks to find organizational change suggests aspects of the literature on incremental budgeting. At the agency level, most budgetary researchers have found results corresponding closely to incrementalism (Davis, Dempster, and Wildavsky, 1966, 1974). When budgets are disaggregated to the program level, however, other researchers have found substantially greater change and unpredictability (Gist, 1977; Natchez and Bupp, 1973). Similarly, if we look at cabinet departments in the United States, we find very little change over centuries; from 1789 to 1987, a total of fifteen creation events have occurred, there has been one major merger and one major split. If we look at clearly identifiable agencies beneath the cabinet level, however, there have been thousands of births, deaths, and transformations (see below). If we were able to examine change at the programmatic level in a thorough manner, there would almost certainly have been tens of thousands of changes. Therefore, where we choose to look to find an organization will determine to a great extent what sorts of results we are likely to obtain.

Let us return now to figure 2 and to a more difficult question for the classification of organizations. Figure 2 displays the organizational chart for HUD, which has many fewer clearly identifiable organizations under its umbrella than does the Department of Agriculture. There are some identifiable organizations, for example, the Government National Mortgage Association, but for the most part HUD is organized around a series of assistant secretaries responsible for a range of programs. If we look more closely beneath that structure, the assistant secretaries supervise a series of program offices (see figure 3). Most of these offices do not have a public law basis, however, and are therefore potentially subject to rapid change with only minimal formalities. HUD is a department organized around programs, and to some extent around its field staff, rather than around more formal organizations within the department.

The HUD structure is important for comparative purposes, for it corresponds rather closely to the structure of administration in most European countries. Figure 4 is my own construction of an organization chart for the Ministry of Agriculture, Fisheries, and Food (MAFF) in the United Kingdom, based upon the *Civil Service Yearbook* for 1984. It shows the relative absence of clearly identifiable organizations beneath the level of the ministry. The structure is even less defined than that of HUD in the United States and appears based more upon the personnel system in operation in British government (undersecretaries must have deputy secretaries to supervise, deputy secretaries must have assistant secretaries, and so on) and upon program structures than upon formal organizations. Administrators at each level are apparently given a certain amount of work to do even if there may be little logical connection among some parts of that work, for example the section of MAFF which deals with "Cereals, Sugar and External Relations." This particular grouping is especially odd, given that most sugar and cereals now come from the Common Market rather than from abroad and that European policy is under a different deputy secretary. In addition, in many and even most instances, very little in the way of a paper trail can be followed when changes occur within a British ministry. It is

Figure 4. Structure of the Ministry of Agriculture, Fisheries, and Food, United Kingdom.

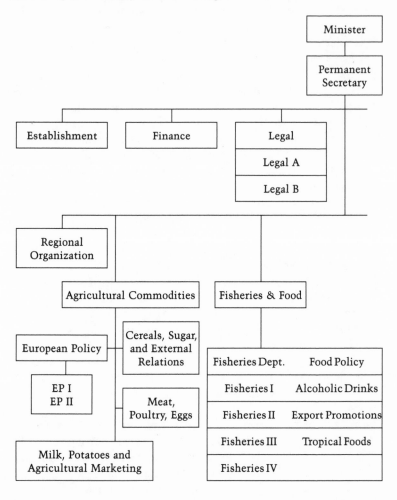

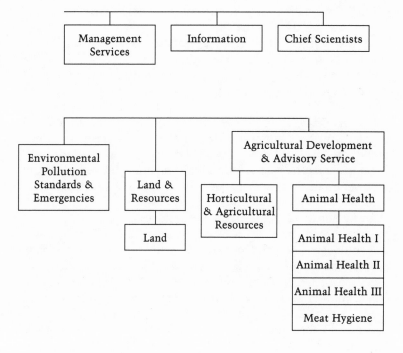

therefore not possible for the researcher to determine when and how organizations, or in this case quasi-organizations, have come into being and passed away. Interestingly, however, the structure of MAFF is better defined than that of many British departments (the Department of Trade and Industry, for example), in which sections are labeled by letter and number (P1, P2, and so forth) rather than by any identifiable piece of work or on any formal legal basis. It should be noted that in MAFF, however, there are sections labeled "Animal Health I, Animal Health II," and so on, without any further designation of the work they are to perform.

In identifying public organizations we may also ask when an organization (assuming that we can clearly identify it) is public and when it is not. To some degree this question is a replay of some of the issues concerning employment that were raised in chapter 2, although here the emphasis is more clearly on *organizations* rather than on individuals, and questions that relate to part-time work do not arise. Somewhat different questions about the fringe of government, which is more evident with organizations than with individuals, do arise, however (Musolf and Seidman, 1980). In particular, it appears much easier to deal with comparative questions by looking at organizations than by enumerating individual employees.

Some organizations, for example, HUD, are clearly public. Its employees are paid from government sources, they are covered by the federal civil service system, they are covered by the Freedom of Information Act, and so on. HUD, however, also has a number of advisory committees (only 4 at last count in contrast to the 250 for the Department of Health and Human Services). These may or may not be assigned civil servants as staff, and the majority of the members will come from the private sector, but they are important for making public policy. Are they public organizations? Even more remote from HUD would be an organization such as the Urban Institute, which was fostered by HUD as a private sector research organization concerned with the policy questions in HUD's area of responsibility. It still does a great deal of work for HUD but also does policy research for other clients. Its employees are not civil servants, but the organization does a great deal of contract research for government. We would probably all agree that the Urban Institute is not a public organization, but it does stand in a rather peculiar position relative to the public sector. The Rand Corporation is in a similar position relative to the Department of Defense. Just as there is a military industrial complex composed of the Department of Defense and its contractors, there is an urban-welfare complex composed of domestic agencies and their hired consultants. Therefore, just as with personnel, we need some means of determining what is a public organization and what is not.

In comparative analysis, some of these interconnections and hybrid forms of organization are extremely important. Take, for example, the organization chart (figure 5) of the Swedish Ministry of Agriculture (Jordbruksdepartment, literally "farmers department"), which was assembled on the basis of information in the *Sveriges Statskalendar*. We can identify three distinct levels of "publicness" in the organizations appearing in that chart. First, there is the ministry itself, which is very much a public organization, although in Swedish public administration the ministries are small and are concerned almost entirely with making and monitoring policy rather than with implementing it. In this case the ministry itself employs only a few hundred people.

At the second level are *styrelsen* (boards) and other similar organizations *(centrala ämbetsverk)* under the tutelage of the ministry but to some degree autonomous as well (Tarschys, 1973; Vinde and Petri, 1975). In Sweden, unlike most other European countries, one can readily identify organizations below the cabinet department (but for France, see Darbel and Schnapper, 1972). The traditional structure of the styrelsen in fact included a collegial body to advise the permanent staff of the organization and to assist in making policies. These organizations perform the major work of implementing public policy in Sweden. Finally, there are the associated bodies of the styrelsen and the ministry which appear to be in part public and in part private. They are, however, officially identified with a particular government organization and may also be involved in

Figure 5. Structure of the Jordbruksdepartment, Sweden.

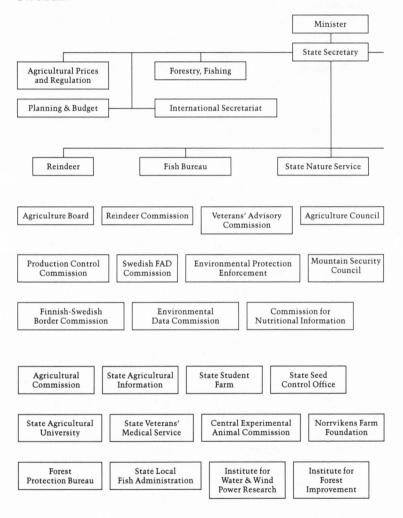

Source: Sveriges Statskalendar (**annual**).

Organizations as Building Blocks

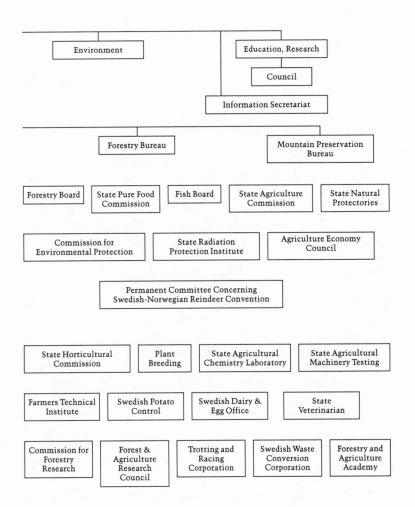

the implementation of policies. This example includes the several firms associated with the forestry board and the agriculture board—are they really public organizations, or are they organizations functioning in the marketplace (Waara, 1980)? Similar links between the public and private sector organizations would be found in virtually all European governments, especially in the Scandinavian countries (Kvavik, 1978) and in Italy, where Instituto per la Ricostruzione Industriale and Ente Nazionale Idrocarburi were very early examples of state holding companies (Pignatelli, 1985).

The distinction between public and private organizations has become a political issue in several countries, most notably the United Kingdom. Even before the Thatcher government initiated a round of "quango-bashing" (Holland, 1981), there was considerable concern about the importance, and apparent lack of accountability, of these quasi-public organizations. In the United Kingdom and other countries, there has been a public hue and cry concerning the role of public corporations and quasi-public corporations and their apparently greater accountability to the market than to government (Feigenbaum, 1985; Vernon, 1984). This difference in accountability is especially pronounced when these firms are created or managed through public holding corporations which may have whole or partial stock ownership but exercise very little direct control over the firms and their activities (Redwood, 1984). In many instances the state will own less than half the stock of a nominally private corporation, although that stock may have been purchased at a time when the new capital was crucial in preventing the company from going bankrupt.

Social security and health insurance systems constitute an interesting, if really unambiguous, case of government's hiving off of important functions and maintaining the legal fiction that they are in essence private organizations. The official public budget in West Germany, France, or a number of other industrialized countries will not mention the social security system. Social security has been relegated to quasi-public organizations. In Germany, for example, there are a number of Krankenkasse, organized by industry or the *Land* for public health insurance. There is no question that the social insurance contributions paid by the German worker and employer are as compulsory as they are in the United States or the United Kingdom, where social insurance schemes are clearly a part of government. The convenient fiction is maintained, however, that the agencies responsible are really private organizations which are in competition and which can bargain with physicians and hospitals without the public sector's being involved directly (Stone, 1980).

The ability to differentiate between public organizations and private organizations is important for several reasons. First, again as in our discussion of personnel, it would be useful to know how large and pervasive government really is. Much of our thinking about "big government" may be based upon erroneous assumptions about size and the meaning of size. In some of the instances cited above, government may be very large, but it is hardly a coordinated Leviathan engaged in taking over the world. Instead, government appears to be terribly disjointed and disorganized and more subject to colonization by the private sector than vice versa. Rather than controlling everything in the economy and society, the authority and control of government are apparently being undermined by the increasing use of quasi-public organizations to do the jobs which one might expect to be performed in the public sector alone.

Second, if we are concerned about a unit of analysis for more empirical, statistical analyses of government structures, then we need some means of enumerating the relevant population. This is very important when, as in the second portion of this chapter, a researcher is interested in the survival and transformation of an entire population of organizations, not just a single organization, or is concerned with obtaining some composite picture of the *structure* of the public sector in a country. This type of research has been done extensively on populations of private sector organizations (Aldrich and Staber, 1986; Carroll and Delacroix, 1982), although relatively little research has yet been done on populations of public sector organizations (but see Casstevens, 1984).

Finally, although we will not dwell on the point here, an understanding of the relationship between public, quasi-public, and private organizations all involved in delivering public services, albeit in different ways, is important for the understanding of public management in the latter portion of the twentieth century (Mosher, 1980; Salamon, 1981a). Government is increasingly government by third parties, by contract, and one step removed. Identification and classification are a first step toward a better understanding of these important changes in the tactics of the state in dealing with policy problems and the surrounding society.

In summary, when we begin trying to define and find government organizations cross-nationally, we confront a number of severe difficulties. In many countries it is difficult to define an organization in any technical or commonsense meaning of the term below the level of the cabinet department. Any attempt to examine the dynamics of a population of organizations therefore provides a very small and misleading number of elements in that population. As we will note shortly, such is not the case in the United States, where we can conduct meaningful research on whole populations of organizations. Moreover, it is difficult to separate public and private organizations, where they are identifiable, from each other. In fact, in countries such as the United Kingdom, quasi-public organizations are apparently much easier to isolate and identify than those that are wholly public. Both sides of the problem present difficulties but ones that we believe it important to address and overcome. The reason is that very interesting and important research can be done using the *organization,* and changes in the population of organizations, as the units of analysis. A good example of such research follows.

The Dynamics of a Population of Public Organizations

Having considered some of the preliminary points about government organizations as the unit of analysis, let us consider an example of research on the population of organizations in the United States federal government. We will provide a very limited amount of comparative research after the more extensive treatment of the research in the United States. The comparative research should indicate that the necessary work can be done readily in some other nations and to some extent, with some perhaps excessively heroic assumptions, in all.

The first theoretical starting point for this research is the book by Herbert Kaufman entitled *Are Government Organizations Immortal?* (1976). This book argued rather strongly that, everything else being equal, government organizations did border on the immortal. In his analysis Kaufman found that only twenty-seven organizations had gone completely out of business in some fifty years. His book has had a great deal of impact, both on scholarship about government and on more practical politics. If indeed a government organization once created is likely to persist, then we should be much more careful in establishing organizations, or at a minimum we should institute procedural safeguards such as sunset laws (Behn, 1978). Furthermore, Kaufman's findings suggest a public sector which is out of control and which will inevitably be increasing in size because nothing goes away and new things are being added in response to technological change or public demand. Finally, if there is such a large body of continuing organizations and programs in government, then the opportunity for innovation and for response to new needs, and to new technologies to "solve" old problems, is limited (Hogwood and Peters, 1983; Tarschys, 1977).

The second point of theoretical departure is the literature, largely stemming from sociology and business, on the population ecology of organizations (Aldrich, 1979; Hannan and Freeman, 1977; McKelvey, 1982). This material examines the births and deaths of organizations using ideas derived from the study of populations of organisms in biology. In particular, there is an assumption that at any one time there will be only so many niches into which organizations can fit in order to survive. If there are too many organizations, or if they are not appropriate for the available niches, they will not survive (Freeman and Hannan, 1983). While this approach is concerned almost entirely with births and deaths rather than with transformations (as is Kaufman), it does provide an interesting approach to understanding the dynamics of organizations in government.

The Simple Dichotomy

Much of the conventional wisdom about the permanence and stability of government organizations is based upon a dichotomous, organic conception of the life cycle of organizations (see McKelvey, 1982): they either live or they die. This view quite obviously fails to take into account the possibility that organizations can change and in changing can transform their forms and functions significantly. While it is popular—and generally correct—to denigrate the use of reorganization as a panacea for the ills of government (March and Olsen, 1983; Salamon, 1981b), change is nevertheless occurring. Organizations may survive, but they may survive in such different forms as to make the term *survival* virtually meaningless. Some analyses of private sector organizations point to a low rate of transformation of organizations (Aldrich and Auster, 1986), but in the public sector transformation appears to be the principal means of change in the population of organizations.

The conventional wisdom with regard to organizational permanence is embodied in Kaufman's book on immortality, a study of persistence of government organizations in the American federal bureaucracy from 1923 to 1973. Kaufman clearly answers the immortality question in the affirmative. In the "sample" of organizations he selected, and using the definition of organizational death which he selected, he found very few terminations over that period. As influential as Kaufman's book has been, and as important as it has been in establishing a research agenda for ourselves and for others, we find it fundamentally flawed. The sample of organizations, the methodology, and the definition of "death" all appear extremely suspect. In fairness it must be said that Kaufman himself recognized some of the problems (1976:30–31, 54) and sought to correct for them in his own discussion of the data. Less sophisticated consumers of his work, however, have tended to accept the findings as an absolute indication of the permanence and stability of government organizations.

The first problem with Kaufman's analysis is the sample of organizations, which comprised agencies from ten of the eleven executive departments existing in 1973. Kaufman explicitly omitted to consider the Department of Defense on the grounds that it was "probably atypical" and would absorb a disproportionate share of the available research resources (1976:25). In my opinion, the additional research effort involved is quite justified for the sake of completeness, and the issue of atypicality is one for empirical testing. Furthermore, as the executive departments represent the principal organizations, and the principal policy concerns, of the federal government, they or their components are less likely ever to be fully terminated. The possibility of functional termination (DeLeon, 1978) is virtually nil. The executive departments and their component organizations constitute, however, a relatively small proportion of all federal organizations (45 percent in 1985). Other federal organizations—even some with relatively large staffs—have been quite ephemeral. To understand the dynamics of organizational change more fully, we should explore a more complete sample.

The second major problem is the methodology that Kaufman employed to determine whether an organizational death had occurred. His procedure was to begin with all organizations existing in 1923, to track all of the organizations until 1973, and then to determine whether they still existed in a recognizable form. This procedure (which might be called middle censorship in the study of biological populations) therefore totally failed to take into account the large number of organizations which came into existence after 1923 and which may have vanished during the time of the inquiry. Empirically, for example, the study ignored the number of organizations that were created during the New Deal and for the most part were terminated as the problems of the depression were "solved" by the onset of World War II. The methodology also ignored the creation of a large number of defense-related organizations and public enterprises during World War II that were terminated at the end of the war. Theoretically, if age is hypothesized to be a factor which will help predict the likelihood that an organization will survive (Freeman, Carroll, and Hannan, 1983; but see Kaufman, 1985; also see Kaufman, 1976), the procedures employed must have excluded from the sample many of the most likely candidates for termination. Therefore, there was a definite bias in the research in favor of finding persistence.

In addition, Kaufman employed a very stringent definition of termination and quite explicitly excluded consideration of the importance of organizational change (1976:26). Kaufman argued that, as long as a boundary around the organization was "uninterruptedly maintained," the organization survived (1976:28). Nystrom and Starbuck (1981:xv–xvi) have criticized this approach and find, using a less stringent definition of termination, that organizational death rates in the public sector correspond closely to those in the private sector. The definition which Nystrom and Starbuck employ, however, groups terminations and changes in organizations together. We believe that for the sake of theoretical development it is very important to maintain the distinction between the two categories. Likewise, in our earlier work on policy change we found a great deal of *change* in federal organizations which would have been counted simply as survival in Kaufman's analysis (Hogwood and Peters, 1983:table 4.1). These changes may mean that organizations simply move from one cabinet department to another or that they undergo more significant changes, none of which were considered by Kaufman's approach. Furthermore these types of changes—which we label organizational successions—appear to constitute an increasing proportion of the total number of organizational activities in the federal bureaucracy. Thus, by selecting as a sample organizations which were most likely to be stable, and by adopting a methodology that concentrated only on dramatic termination events, Kaufman's research presented a picture of stability quite different from the more turbulent picture of the federal bureaucracy that would emerge if a somewhat different approach were taken.

Concepts and Sampling

The research to be reported here uses a much larger sample of organizations—indeed all identifiable organizations in the federal bureaucracy—and separately identifies and analyzes all types of change. It provides a much more complete picture of the federal bureaucracy and demonstrates far more change and turbulence than the conventional wisdom might indicate.

Our own earlier work on policy change provides a more detailed conceptual basis from which to approach the problem of stability or change in populations of government organizations (Hogwood and Peters, 1983). The most important addition to the simple dichotomy of stability and termination is the idea of policy (or organizational) succession. We define succession as the "act by which a previous policy, program or organization is replaced by a 'new' one directed at the same problem and/or clientele" (Hogwood and Peters, 1983:17–18). Using this approach, and being sensitive to the possibility of change without termination, we can reach a much better understanding of the manner in which the public bureaucracy in the United States has evolved over the past half century.

Succession is not an undifferentiated concept. Rather, we have identified a number of different types of change.

Initiations.
The formation of an entirely new organization, typically in an area in which government has not previously been active.

Maintenance.
The continuation of an existing organization with the same task definition and structure.

Termination.
The abolition of an organization with no replacement organization being established.

Succession.
The replacement of an organization by a "new" one directed at the same problem or clientele. This may occur in one of the following ways.

(a) *Linear replacement.* The direct replacement of one organization with another addressed to the same problem but with different goals or methods;

(b) *Consolidation.* The complete or partial termination of two or more organizations and their replacement with a single organization;

(c) *Splitting.* The division of a single existing organization into two or more components;

(d) *Partial termination.* The termination of some aspect of an organization while the remainder of the organization continues to function;

(e) *Nonlinear replacement.* A new organization formed where the purpose is closely related to previous organizations but for which the goals programs and/or structural features may be quite different;

(f) *Complex replacement.* Patterns of change involving some or all of the types of succession above.

As our list shows, these forms of change range from simple linear successions, in which one organization is directly replaced by another, or in which an organization is modified while retaining its basic integrity, to more complex changes involving a number of organizations. Each type of change has somewhat different implications for the organizations involved as well as for their clients. A simple linear replacement, for example, will give clients (relatively) little difficulty, and many of the same staff may continue doing exactly what they had been doing prior to the change, while a partial termination may call into question the entire existence of any organization. We will not discuss all the implications of each type of change here; it is more important to consider the possibility of organizational change while the basic structures themselves persist. This concern with change, in turn, implies a definition of termination not dissimilar from that used by Kaufman. The difference is that we count changes as well as terminations rather than assuming that the absence of complete termination implies the persistence of exactly the same structure.

Hypotheses

We have developed several preliminary hypotheses about persistence and change in the population of public organizations on the basis of Kaufman (1976), Nystrom and Starbuck (1981), Meyer, Stevenson, and Webster (1984), and Hogwood and Peters (1983). These hypotheses are:

1. The rate of *total change* in government organizations is much higher than the rate of total terminations reported by Kaufman.
2. The rate of organizational change has not remained constant across time but has responded to changes in the environment of government. In addition, organizational successions have become an increasingly large component of total change.
3. Organizations which are components of executive departments will be more stable than other types of organizations, for example, independent executive agencies and boards and commissions.
4. Organizations established by statute are more stable than organizations established by other means, for example, executive orders.

Data Base and Methodology

Given the discussion about the difficulties in identifying and classifying government organizations which preceded this empirical analysis, we need to justify the particular definitions of organizations in the federal government which we will be using. In the first place, we will attempt to be inclusive and will therefore encompass advisory bodies, commissions, and so on which exist at the "margins of the state" within this population. The principal test will be whether or not they are listed in the *United States Government Manual* or in *Federal Advisory Committees—Annual Report to the President*. Inclusion of the latter group is justified because they *are* public bodies, established by the president and/or Congress, carry on public business, and frequently employ civil servants to do so. Multinational organizations listed in the *Government Manual*, such as the World Health Organization and the Pan-American Health Organization, have been excluded.

Within larger organizations we needed some rules as to what constituted an organization and what did not. In general, we worked by exclusion. First, we did not include the field structure of organizations or individual installations as separate organizations. Also, in general we did not go more than three levels down in an organization (for example, department, agency, bureau). The data below that level are extremely inconsistent, and since very few, if any, organizations below that level would have any sort of basis in public law, it seemed reasonable to halt our investigation at the third tier. Finally, entries on organization charts which were personalized (for example, assistant secretary for something or the other) had to be investigated quite thoroughly. Some such entries do have definite and important organizational manifestations, while others appear to consist of the individual and a very small personal staff. We might usefully contrast the assistant secretary of defense for manpower, logistics, and installations with a very large organization having assistant secretaries for administration in several departments with little or no organizational structures surrounding them.

The definition of our sample involves the enumeration of organizations existing within organizations. All the agencies and bureaus displayed in figure 1 exist within the structure of the Department of Agriculture. They are no less organizations, however, especially given the tendency of the American public bureaucracy to build on the agency base rather than on a departmental base (Seidman and Gilmour, 1986). The major attendant problem is a decision as to whether each change occurring within, for example, the Farmers Home Administration counts as both a change in that agency and a change in the Department of Agriculture. We decided to count such a change as a *single* event in this particular analysis, although if we were to focus more directly on cabinet departments we might perform the analysis differently. Counting such changes twice in the present instance would exaggerate the amount of change that has occurred. In addition, this is the level of organization with which Kaufman worked, and by using this approach we make our results more comparable to his. Finally, the comparative nature of the research can be enhanced by this approach, which resembles that used by previous scholarly work (Darbel and Schnapper, 1972).

While these definitions of organizations may not be totally satisfying, they do provide a means of obtaining a consistent and largely inclusive set of organizations. In this particular analysis, however, we are interested more in *changes* in the population of organizations than in actual enumeration of the organizations themselves at any one time. The data to address research questions concerning change can be drawn from the *United States Government Manual*. The data consist of information on every change in the structures of government from March 4, 1933, to July 1, 1985. These data are to be found in Appendix A of the 1984–1985 *Manual*. In addition, we have been through the body of the *Manual* itself, as well as through annual reports of many government organizations, in order to attempt to capture every change in organizations during the period. The data to be reported here are coded as *events*—for example, an initiation of an organization, a termination, or one type or another of organizational succession.

The data base consists of 2,245 events which arose from 889 organizations. In enumerating events we took an obviously different approach from that employed by Kaufman. It is, however, a more flexible approach which will permit us both to track organizations through time, as Kaufman did, and to develop profiles of total organizational activity in government. Furthermore, if these events were weighted with budgetary and personnel information (an analysis not to be reported here) the data can address questions about how "big government" in the United States has come into being. Even without such weighting, however, the data do show how the structure of government has been adapting to increased demands and an increased workload.

Several problems which arose in the methodology should be mentioned here. One is the fundamental problem of coding. Only two people did all of the coding, but some decisions involved in coding were inevitably matters of judgment as to whether one particular type of change rather than another had occurred. The vast majority of the ambiguities, however, were between different types of successions—especially consolidations and nonlinear changes—rather than between successions and other types of changes. Hence we are confident that the enumeration of the three major categories of change is accurate.

In several of the analyses we will examine changes occurring in different decades. In interpreting these tables, the reader should remember that the 1930s include only the period 1933–1939, the only years for which we have data, while the 1970s include the early 1980s as well, since as yet there are too few entries in the 1980s to permit separate analysis. Our future plans are to extend the analysis to explore change in government organizations in different and more precise time periods, for example the terms of office of different presidents (Peters and Hogwood, forthcoming).

Findings

We made a tentative empirical analysis related to the four hypotheses outlined above. The rather low level of statistical analysis may make some of the more sophisticated members of our profession cringe, but even these simple percentages tell a great deal about change in this complex environment.

As we have been arguing in this chapter and elsewhere (Hogwood and Peters, 1983), the idea that public sector organizations are stable, while widely accepted, appears to be incorrect. Our first hypothesis was that the total rate of change in public organizations would be substantially higher than the mortality rate reported by Kaufman. The summary of our findings for total change for the period of 1933 to 1984 confirms that hypothesis quite strongly (table 10). During this period there were

Table 10. Types of Policy Change by Decade (percent)

	1930s	1940s	1950s	1960s	1970s	Total
Initiation	33	32	49	48	33	37
Termination	8	13	17	13	16	14
Succession (total)	59	55	34	39	51	49
Linear replacement	48	37	23	24	30	35
Consolidation	8	13	8	7	16	11
Splitting	1	3	1	4	2	2
Nonlinear replacement	1	2	1	3	2	1
Partial termination	1	1	1	1	1	1
Total	100	100	100	100	101	101
N	442	562	294	349	598	2,245

Source: Office of the Federal Register (1984).

2,245 changes in the population of organizations in the federal government, including initiations, terminations, and successions. Of the total, 37 percent were organizational initiations, 14 percent were organizational terminations, and 49 percent were organizational successions of various types. Interestingly, the percentage of terminations is almost exactly the same as that found by Kaufman (14 percent versus 15 percent). The major difference is that these are *events* rather than organizations, and hence the ratio to the number of organizations would be much higher in our data. If we relate the 306 terminations in our data to the 889 organizations which were identified, for example, the percentage of terminations would be increased to 34 percent, a figure closer to that found by Nystrom and Starbuck, using their somewhat different methodology (1981). It should be noted, however, that a large share of the terminations were in advisory and nonexecutive bodies. Furthermore, the percentage does not take into account the large number of organizational successions. From these data it is clear that, while government may appear permanent and stable, a great deal of organizational change is occurring just beneath the calm surface.

As hypothesized, the rate of change in the population of gov-

Table 11. Rates of Total Activity by Policy Area
(percentage of total activity in policy area)

	1930s	1940s	1950s	1960s	1970s
Public Works	2	26	16	3	3
Agriculture	31	20	12	11	26
Commerce	38	23	8	9	22
Defense	2	60	19	6	13
International Affairs	7	31	18	23	21
Housing/Urban Affairs	17	33	10	20	20
Welfare	12	10	8	40	30
Education	10	14	14	22	40
Transportation	17	16	17	30	20
Natural Resources	24	14	7	20	35
Economic Policy	7	20	14	19	34
Health	4	23	8	17	48
Energy	14	15	11	4	56
Justice	15	11	13	15	46
Environment	—	—	—	31	69
Other	22	10	17	16	35

Source: Office of the Federal Register (1982).

ernment organizations was not constant over the fifty years
(see table 11). The 1940s and the 1970s-1980s were most active
periods, having together almost half the total number of
changes. The 1950s, on the other hand, were the least active
years. These patterns may be explained in part by the impact of
World War II and the declining need for New Deal agencies in
the 1940s and the generally increased level of activism of the
federal government in the 1970s. In the latter regard, it should
be noted that there were almost as many initiations of organizations in the 1960s as in the 1970s-1980s; these initiations
appeared to have set the stage for a large number of successions
in the 1970s-1980s period (Peters and Hogwood, 1985). The
1950s were largely dominated by the Eisenhower administration, which was not as active as many others in either policy
terms or organizational terms (but see Greenstein, 1982).

On the other hand, the 1950s had the highest rate of termina-

tions (as a percentage of total activity), followed closely by the
1970s-1980s. Much of the termination in the 1950s was in the
area of defense (fifteen terminations of forty-seven) and represented the return of the defense establishment to a peacetime
(or Cold War) status after its expansion during World War II and
the Korean conflict. The terminations of the 1970s and 1980s
were spread more evenly among policy areas, with the largest
single area of activity being the general category of "other activities of government." There was substantial activity in the
areas of the environment and natural resources. These latter
two categories encompass some of the activities of the Reagan
administration, in the person of James Watt in the early 1980s.
Not all the terminations in this latter time period were by any
means the work of the Reagan administration, however; President Carter was also reasonably active in paring down the size
of the federal government.

Elsewhere we have argued that we would expect to find an
increasing proportion of successions as a component of total
policy and organizational activity (Hogwood and Peters, 1983).
That assertion is substantiated when the 1970s-1980s are compared to the 1950s and 1960s but not when they are compared
to earlier decades. The high level of activity in the earlier decades is the result of the federal government's attempts to cope
with the problems of the depression and World War II in the
1930s and 1940s. Of a total of 310 successions in the 1940s,
for example, 113 are in the area of defense. Likewise, of the
252 successions in the 1930s, 69 are in agriculture and commerce—many of which were New Deal organizations being
reorganized to meet changing conditions and changing conceptions of how to produce economic recovery.

There has, therefore, been a great deal more change in governmental structure and in the population of public organizations than would have been expected, given the conventional
wisdom. This statement is true both for organizational terminations and for the various types of the changes in organizations we have been terming successions. On the one hand, one
might argue that many of these organizations have survived,
but on the other hand they appear to have survived in such

different forms that the term *survival* becomes somewhat meaningless.

Several characteristics of public organizations have been hypothesized to relate to their relative stability. One characteristic is the type of organization. The organizational zoo of the federal government comprises a number of different types of animals (Moe, 1980; Seidman and Gilmour, 1986). They include agencies in cabinet departments, independent executive agencies, independent regulatory commissions, organizations within the executive office of the president, public corporations, boards and commissions, and a host of other types of organizations. In order to simplify the analysis somewhat, and to give us sufficiently large numbers for comparison, we have coded all organizations into four categories: agencies of cabinet departments, independent agencies (including both executive and regulatory bodies), agencies in the executive office of the president, and other organizations (mostly boards and commissions).

Kaufman's work excluded all federal organizations except agencies within cabinet departments, but in this study we include all types of organizations. We might expect the bulk of change, particularly termination, to occur in organizations other than those in the cabinet departments. These departments are the major components of the federal government and represent long-standing commitments to provide certain types of services; the component agencies accounted for 45 percent of all federal organizations in 1985. The implication is not that these organizations are necessarily immortal, of course, but that less change should be expected.

At the other end of the immortality spectrum, organizations established as boards, commissions, advisory councils, and so on should be expected to be the shortest lived of government organizations and to contribute disproportionately to total organizational activity, especially termination. Such bodies are frequently given a time period within which to complete their work and then automatically go out of existence unless they are reauthorized. The idea of the "sunset law" has been discussed in the United States since the mid-1970s (Behn, 1978),

Table 12. Change in Each Type of Organization (percent)

Change	N	Departments	Independent	Executive office of the president	Commissions	Total
		Analysis by Type of Organization				
Initiations	—	37	35	48	43	39
Terminations	—	8	10	26	30	15
Successions	—	55	55	26	27	47
Total	—	100	100	100	100	101
N		739	451	111	403	1,704
		Analysis by Type of Organizational Change				
Initiations	657	42	24	8	26	100
Terminations	254	23	18	11	48	100
Successions	793	51	31	4	13	99
Percentage of total		43	26	7	24	100
Total N	1,704	—	—	—	—	—

Source: Peters and Hogwood (forthcoming).

but in many specific instances it has been in place for a number of years. As with agencies in cabinet departments, however, commissions and boards are not an undifferentiated whole, and some organizations which begin life as temporary bodies live to a ripe old age.

Table 12 summarizes our findings for each type of organizational change for the four types of organizations. The first thing to be noted is that the largest single source of organizational change was agencies in the cabinet departments. Most of these changes, however, were successions. The agencies accounted for 45 percent of the stock of government organizations in 1984 but for only 23 percent of all terminations. In contrast, cabinet agencies accounted for more than half the total number of successions; their survival has involved changes. Departmental agencies thus change as often as the average organization, but they die less frequently, and an analysis focusing only on their survival would tend to find permanence (Kaufman, 1976).

Organizational changes within independent executive and regulatory agencies demonstrate some interesting patterns. Although similar to the cabinet agencies as a proportion of the total stock of organizations in 1984 (46 percent), independent agencies accounted for only 26 percent of all changes. Within the total changes, independent agencies show a distribution among initiations, terminations, and successions broadly similar to that for cabinet agencies. This statement conceals an important change across time, however. Independent agencies in the 1930s accounted for a higher proportion of changes than did the cabinet agencies. Within the total, independent agencies accounted for an even higher percentage of initiations. Since that time the pattern has changed dramatically, with independent agencies accounting for fewer than half the number of changes occurring in the cabinet agencies. Within the total, there has been a further significant change: in the 1930s, 48 percent of changes in the independent agencies were initiations, and 45 percent were successions; in the 1970s-1980s, only 27 percent of changes have been initiations, while 66 percent were successions. Terminations rose as a percentage of changes between the 1930s and 1950s but fell back to the 1930s level again by the 1970s. By the 1970s, independent agencies had the appearance of being more stable than the cabinet agencies and of having a disproportionately high ratio of successions to all changes.

Although units of the executive office of the president (EOP) were only 1 percent of the 1984 stock of organizations, they have accounted for 7 percent of the total number of changes during the time period. Similarly, commissions and so forth, while only 7 percent of the 1984 stock of organizations, have accounted for 24 percent of the total changes. For both types of organization, initiations and terminations were a substantially higher proportion of changes (terminations three times higher) than they were for cabinet agencies and independent agencies. Commissions and so on accounted for nearly half of all termination events in the data set, confirming the expectation that they have a shorter life.

The frequency of initiation and termination changes in the EOP reflects the desire of every president to run his own personal office in his own way and the greater discretion he has in making these changes. The rate of change for commissions reflects the limited time span of the tasks most are given, although there are some examples of commissions that become permanent fixtures in government, for example the President's Council on Physical Fitness. Some interesting changes have occurred over time in the proportion of each type of change for these two types of organization. The proportion of terminations in the EOP has risen steadily over time, reflecting in part the fact that the EOP was not formed until 1939. There has been a marked drop from 65 percent in the 1950s to 38 percent in the 1970s-1980s in the proportion of changes which are initiations. Among commissions, there was a switch in the proportion of initiations and terminations between the 1960s and 1970s from 48 percent initiations and 29 percent terminations to 28 percent and 49 percent. In other words, fewer were born and more died.

The continuing importance of change, including initiations, within the cabinet departments, does raise a question about the often repeated assertion that government tends to develop peripheral organizations (Sharkansky, 1979; Walsh, 1978). Clearly, a definitive treatment of this question would require a more refined set of coding categories and analysis of changes in the relative sizes of organizations, but our preliminary findings do suggest that change in the heartland of government has been underemphasized, at least for the United States, in the recent literature.

Kaufman (1976:42–47) explored the extent to which an organization's survival is affected by the authority under which it is created. His finding was that "statutory bodies were no more likely to escape elimination than agencies dependent upon other legal instruments" (p. 42). We will examine this hypothesis within our larger set of organizations while at the same time differentiating between successions, terminations, and simple stability. Organizations are coded as having been organized on the basis of statutes (acts or joint resolutions of Congress), executive orders from the president, orders from a cabinet secretary or other administrative officer, a reorganization plan, or some other basis (a letter from the president, for example).

One might expect the establishment of a completely new organization to be more likely to be accomplished through statutes than by any other means and a statutory basis to provide greater protection against termination. As can be seen from table 13, however, statutes accounted for only 35 percent of all initiations from 1933 to 1984, slightly less than the proportion accounted for by presidential orders (37 percent). In contrast, statute-based organizations account for a substantially higher proportions of terminations (45 percent). Far from providing protection against termination, a statutory basis appears to make organizations *more* termination prone than average. A similar, though less marked tendency can be found for organizations established by presidential orders, with 40 percent of all terminations occurring in this category.

Reorganization plans demonstrate some tendency to produce organizations which are themselves subsequently reorganized rather than terminated: there were 15 times as many

Table 13. Types of Organizational Change in Organizations with Different Bases (percent)

Change	Statute	Presidential order	Secretary's order	Reorganization plan	Total
Analysis by Organizational Basis					
Initiations	32	43	39	37	—
Terminations	19	21	10	4	—
Successions	49	36	51	59	—
Total	100	100	100	100	—
N	688	552	405	54	1,699
Analysis by Type of Change					
Initiations	35	37	25	3	100
Terminations	45	40	14	1	100
Successions	44	26	27	4	101
Percentage of total	41	32	24	3	100
N	688	552	405	54	1,699

Note: For initiations the basis of organization refers to the instrument by which the new organization is established. For terminations and successions the basis of organization refers to the basis on which the organization was originally established and not to the instrument through which termination or succession was brought about.
Source: Peters and Hogwood (forthcoming).

subsequent successions as terminations (compared with 2.5 times as many for statute-based organizations, 1.5 times as many for organizations produced by presidential orders, and 5 times as many for organizations resulting from other executive orders). There may be several reasons for these apparently strange findings. First, many organizations founded by statute are the commissions mentioned above, and they often have a sunset provision as a part of their initial legislation. In addition, the president may form organizations with a limited lifetime, as is reflected by the high proportion of terminations in this category. In addition, it might be argued that organizations formed by an act of Congress would, everything else being equal, be more innovative than organizations formed on some other basis. The federal government becomes involved in a policy area for the first time usually as the result of an act of Congress rather than because of initiative taken by a cabinet secretary or even by the president. On the other hand, cabinet secretaries may be given a good deal of latitude in modifying the established programs and organizations within their departments. Since Congress is, as it were, gambling when it forms a new organization, there will probably be some mistakes, and some organizations initiated will be terminated. Likewise, the parts of government which would be included in a reorganization plan are more likely to be tried-and-true functions of government which may have to be altered again later but would be less likely to be terminated.

There have been some variations in the patterns of change within these categories across time. For organizations formed by statutes and organizations formed by presidential orders, terminations have become a much higher proportion of all organizational changes. Terminations as a proportion of the total number of events have doubled for both categories. In addition, in the 1930s 41 percent of all organizational initiations were statute-based, while in the 1970s this figure was reduced to 34 percent. On the other hand, in the 1930s, 15 percent of all initiations were by executive order, and this figure has increased to 22 percent. The share of initiations by the president was almost the same in the two decades. These findings would appear to indicate somewhat greater delegation of organizational powers to administrators, a feature which has certainly been frequently ascribed to government in the 1970s and 1980s.

There are relatively slight differences in the types of successions which each type of organization (classified by the basis of their formation) tends to undergo. The major difference is that organizations founded by administrative officers tend to have a higher proportion of consolidations than do other types of organizations. This difference would be logical, given that it would be natural for a cabinet secretary to react to a problem in his or her own area of competence by establishing an organization. The organization might later be joined with other organizations to improve coordination and (possibly) efficiency.

In summary, formation by an act of Congress is not the talisman against termination that it is sometimes considered. Organizations formed on this basis actually contribute more terminations to the total than do organizations with an apparently less firm basis in law. The reason appears in large part to be the built-in terminators in some of the legislation passed by Congress as well as the more innovative nature of some of the policy and organizational initiations undertaken by statutes (see, for example, Polsby, 1984). The legislative process appears, however, to be losing its role as the initiator of organizational change; a declining number of new organizations are being formed by statutes.

If nothing else, the analysis has demonstrated that assumptions about stability in government organizations—at least in the United States—are poorly founded or may be artifacts of the sample and methodology selected. A great deal of change has occurred in government over the fifty-year period we investigated. This change has included the birth of new organizations, the death of many more than might have been anticipated, and the metamorphoses of even more. The machinery of government appears to be constantly adapting to new demands, ideas, and political priorities rather than standing still. We believe that the conceptual apparatus we have developed allows us to capture the movement in a more meaningful fashion than was possible before. While dramatic termination or initiation events are certainly important, the modal change in government is actually the transformation of existing organizations and probably of existing policies as well.

We have also illustrated the utility of organizations as a unit of analysis in the study of government and particularly the utility of using whole populations. The analysis of these populations can give an idea of the structure of government or, in this particular case, of changes in the structure. Furthermore, as some earlier work has demonstrated (Peters and Hogwood, 1985), organizations can be used to analyze something of the changing priorities of governments.

Some Limited Comparisons

As we noted before embarking on the rather lengthy analysis of change in the U.S. federal bureaucracy, we do want to make at least some limited comparisons with other countries. We have already noted that such comparisons are difficult because of the less clearly articulated organizational structures of many other industrialized countries. France and Sweden are two countries (Canada is a third) in which direct comparisons of change can be made readily. These countries have identifiable organizational subunits with some legal life of their own, although (especially in France) not as clearly defined as in the United States.

Perhaps the simplest form of analysis of the development of organizational populations has already been performed for France. Darbel and Schnapper (1972:63–65) tracked the development of the ministries in French government from the 1790s to 1966. Even at that high a level of aggregation, it is easy to detect many of the same types of organizational events we have identified in the United States. Using the materials Darbel and Schnapper present, we can identify six initiations of ministries; most ministries created later are split off from existing ministries (especially from Intérieur). During the same period, lasting more than a century and a half, there were some forty-seven successions at the ministerial level. These successions involved mostly splits and linear changes of functions from one ministry to another, but some consolidations (frequently just prior to a split) could also be identified. Even at a very high level of aggregation, we can see how the individuals responsible for the populations of organizations attempted to adapt to meet changes in demands ("niches") and in politics. (For somewhat similar, although less quantifiable, analyses in the United Kingdom, see Chester and Willson, 1968, and Pollitt, 1984).

Darbel and Schnapper (1972:190–91) were also interested in the articulation of public organizations in the face of changing demands and work loads. They counted the number of decision units within ministries beginning in 1870 and continuing until the 1930s. Using the *Bottin Administratif* (Didot-Bottin, annual), we have been able to extend this analysis until the late 1970s. Using the six ministries that existed with the same name and in roughly the same form in 1978 as they did in the 1930s, we see, as might be expected, a significant expansion in the number of decision units (see table 14). Also interesting is the way in which the departments have retained their own particular organizational styles. The Ministry of Agriculture in the 1930s, and even in the early twentieth century, for example, had a relatively large number of bureaus relative to other decision centers, while the Ministry of Foreign Affairs depended less on bureaus than on other forms of decision centers. This tendency persists into the present, although the tendency of the Ministry of Agriculture to create bureaus has been even more exaggerated. These differences may make good administrative sense; more high-level coordination may be needed in making foreign policy than in making agricultural policy. The differences may, however, also reflect the persistence of distinctive administrative styles and cultures in the ministries.

Resources have prevented us from undertaking a complete analysis of organizational change in Sweden, but we have performed some analysis of changes which have occurred in one cabinet department (our old friend the Jordbruksdepartment) for the period 1932 to 1982. The data were drawn by the authors from *Sveriges Statskalendar*, an annual publication sim-

Table 14. Development of Decision Centers in French Ministries, 1870–1978

	1870		1900		1925		1936		1978	
	Total[a]	Bureaux	Total	Bureaux	Total	Bureaux	Total	Bureaux	Total	Bureaux
Foreign affairs	14	3	33	20	26	7	34	20	71	25
Agriculture	26	15	21	14	27	18	30	21	229	164
Justice	17	12	18	14	20	15	21	17	60	41
Industry	NA	NA	19	14	27	19	30	23	71	46
Interior	50	37	40	34	22	17	30	24	56	46

Note: NA = not available.
[a]*Directions, sous-directions, services,* and *bureaux.*
Sources: Darbel and Schnapper (1972:190–91); Didot-Bottin (1978).

ilar to the *U.S. Government Manual.* As with the analysis of
the United States, we will examine an inclusive group of organizations associated with this department, including some
which might better be considered quasi-governmental.

Table 15. Rates of Organizational Activity in the Swedish
Agriculture Department, 1932–1982

	Initiations	Terminations	Successions Linear	Split	Consolidation	Total
1932–52	12	4	5	6	4	15
1952–72	5	4	3	3	5	11
1972–82	8	5	4	10	3	17

Source: Sveriges Statskalendar (annual).

Table 15 provides some evidence of the changes which have
occurred in this organization. Given the smaller number of
cases from a single department, longer time periods have been
used than for the United States. We see roughly similar patterns of organizational activity, however. In the first place,
there have been a significant number of changes, and there
have been changes of all types—initiations, terminations, and
successions. In fact, the termination rate has been somewhat
higher than in the United States. This result might not have
been anticipated, given that Sweden has been considered a
model of the welfare state and of a large public sector, while the
United States is usually considered in general to have an anti-
governmental ideology. In addition, the rate of successions has
been increasing, much as people have argued that it should in
any advanced industrialized society when government begins
to accumulate a number of commitments and programs and
most policymaking becomes tinkering with the existing programs.

There were, however, a number of successions in the earliest
of the three time periods. As with the United States, many of
them represented changes in programs designed to cope with

the depression. Also, the relatively large number of successions in the latest time period appears to be the product of a relatively small number of quite important initiations in the 1950s and 1960s, when the agricultural organization became more heavily involved in environmental protection and consumer protection. Much of the organizational activity from the late 1970s onward represents the ramification (note the number of splits) of these relatively new types of organizations within this department.

Another interesting point here is that the initiations in the last time period correspond more closely to the view of the development of government put forward by Sharkansky (1979) and others concerned with the "margins of the State" (1979:3) Most of these initiations occurred at the tertiary level in the department (see above), and several were quasi-public firms which were as much in the marketplace as in government. It would appear that, while organizations which are clearly governmental are somewhat slow to change at present, there is great activity on the margins. In both Sweden and France, as in the United States, there is a great deal of organizational activity, and the structure of government has been greatly altered over the decades being researched.

Conclusion

This chapter began with a discussion of the utility of organizations as units of analysis in the study of government. It also noted the difficulty of identifying all the relevant units in a population of government organizations. The difficulties spring from the uncertainty as to what an organization is in government and as to which organizations that can be identified are actually public.

Although the United States has all the difficulties we discussed, it is still an easier environment in which to do research on government organizations than are most other countries. The tendency to define organizations by a legal act of some nature, and to identify them *as* organizations, makes the task of the researcher somewhat more manageable than it would be in most European countries with very fluid and ill-defined organizational structures below the level of the cabinet department. There organizations appear to come and go almost at the will of incumbent governments or ministers and leave very little trace for the researcher to follow.

We explored the possibility of doing organizational research on the U.S. federal bureaucracy in conducting a detailed analysis of organizational change in the United States from the time of the New Deal almost to the present. This analysis revealed a great deal of organizational activity—much more than might have been imagined by the conventional wisdom stressing the permanence and immutability of government organizations. Identification of this change, however, involves a conceptual framework which differentiates between change and terminations and therefore permits us to discern organizational changes other than dramatic termination or creation events. This research can be used to illustrate how government—at a minimum in the United States—has been growing (at least in terms of the number of units in government) and changing since the 1930s and, then, to make some observations about directions of future change. Although the possibilities of directly comparable research may be limited in some countries, the research does indicate one means of attacking the data problem in comparative public administration. Furthermore, with great attention to detail, and perhaps with some access to files and information other than official listings of organizations, it may be possible to do such research even in countries such as the United Kingdom where is now appears impossible.

Apart from being of academic interest, this organizational research also addresses important issues of more practical politics. It provides one set of answers to the question of how expansion in the public sector may have occurred and also to the question of how that sector does change. Conservatives have liked to argue that government is some sort of Leviathan which will perpetually increase in size because once involved in an issue area it will never leave of its own accord. These data suggest that there are relatively few functional terminations by government but that there are a great many more organizational terminations that might have been imagined and certainly greater change within bureaucracy. The public bureaucracy is not the immortal and rigid entity it is conventionally thought to be. It is important to understand change, and the means of producing desired change, rather than to wait for the inevitable expansion of government.

4

The Behavior
of
Public Officials

A bureaucrat has no option but to be an anarchist or an idiot.

Anonymous

The third of our possible dependent variables for the study of public administration is the behavior of public officials in administrative positions. I earlier blamed the relatively poor condition of comparative public administration in large measure on the success of the behavioral revolution in political science. In fairness, however, it should be noted that this revolution opened some new doors for research at the same time that it closed many others and, most important, tended to direct attention away from administration.

In particular, the behavioral approach alerted us to the simple fact that different individuals may be expected to behave differently in public office and that not all occupants of formal positions in a hierarchy follow the rules of that hierarchy. While students of private sector organizations had known these simple truths for some years, for example, through concepts such as that of the informal organization (Roethlisberger and Dickson, 1939), these insights were a revelation to some students of public administration, largely because of the dominance of Weberian, Wilsonian, and other formalistic approaches to government. These approaches emphasized legal compliance rather than discretion or decisionmaking on the part of public administrators. The possibility that public administrators showed real behavioral differences then constituted a new avenue for research in public administration and offered a different understanding of how the organizations within government really worked.

This open door for research has been inviting but has been extremely difficult to pass through. The study of behavior within public organizations is difficult, especially when one undertakes comparative studies. This statement is true for several reasons. The first is the simple problem of access. Relatively few public administrators are willing to give researchers the kind of access that Kaufman (1981b), for example, had when he spent some months sitting in the office of six federal bureau chiefs, recording their behavior while they carried on with their jobs. Even if the researcher does not seek direct access to decisionmaking, the types of decisions that senior civil servants must make are potentially so politically sensitive that the civil servants may be unwilling to discuss them. Discussion may be possible after the civil servants leave office, as students of British politics in particular have discovered, but for some purposes that may be too late. It may be more possible to observe directly, or to ask questions about, lower-echelon civil servants whose work is less sensitive but is certainly important for the implementation of policy. Research in the lower echelons will not, however, answer many of the questions which students of public organizations have posed for themselves.

As well as having difficulty with gaining access, a researcher in public administration may find it hard to understand the context of decisions and behavior. Despite their best efforts, most researchers in public administration will not be able to comprehend completely the complex and subtle world within which senior civil servants function. Again, this statement is especially true when comparative studies are being undertaken. Slight differences in wording, or a single sentence in a memorandum, may make a profound difference for a particular decision. It is extremely difficult for outsiders to understand these nuances or the nuances of behavior which may have produced them. This problem could be taken to the extreme, as logical extensions of the action approach to social phenomena might treat it (Harmon, 1981), to make comparative research almost impossible. Even if such an extreme approach is not adopted, comparative research on administrative behavior is demanding although not necessarily impossible. Some fine pieces of research, such as Heclo and Wildavsky (1974) on the British Treasury, Suleiman's work (1974, 1978, 1985) on French bureaucracy, Olsen's work (1983; see also Laegreid and Olsen, 1978) in Norway, and Campbell and Szablowski's directly comparative research (1979) on central agencies in several countries, demonstrate the possibilities.

Finally, there is the methodological problem of the reactive effects of most situations in which one might want to research administrative behavior (Campbell and Stanley, 1963; Webb et al., 1966). The researcher is always an outsider, except in the rare instances when a participant in the process is also the observer (examples would be Barnett, 1982; Good, 1980; Pliatzky, 1982). Therefore, it is possible that those being observed might behave differently from the way they would behave when they were not being observed, even when interviewing rather than direct observation is the means of data collection. For many questions that a civil servant might be asked, some answers are more socially acceptable than others. Unlike the direct observation of behavior, these methods may be more important for lower echelons of the civil service than for upper echelons. Most civil servants probably know how they are supposed to treat their clients; the question is, how do they really treat those clients? Even when clients are being questioned about the behavior of civil servants toward them, the clients may be under some pressure to provide favorable reports. They may perceive themselves as being in powerless positions and be afraid to give negative reports about civil servants for fear of losing benefits. All these factors combine to make it quite difficult to gather unbiased and reliable information about the behavior of civil servants.

Possible Concepts and Variables

Having now demonstrated the difficulty of doing proper research on the behavior of members of the public bureaucracy,

I will now proceed to discuss some possible ways of doing such research. This attempt to do research is not inconsistent, but is intended to be realistic while at the same time being optimistic. If social scientists avoided all research questions which presented methodological and practical problems, little or no social research would be conducted.

Relationships with Clients

We can begin to examine the behavior of civil servants at the point at which they relate to the world outside the public bureaucracy. One of the most important questions about the conduct of public bureaucracy, especially in liberal, democratic political systems with well-developed concepts of administrative accountability, concerns the way in which civil servants relate to the clients they are intended to serve. I have already noted that, despite the emphasis on the upper echelons of bureaucracy in most studies of the public sector, the very lowest echelons of public organizations exercise a great deal of discretion. In addition, this discretion is important for determining what really happens in government. The cop on the beat, the schoolteacher, the welfare worker, the tax inspector, and all the other public officials who come into contact with citizens help to define the reality of government for those citizens (Kaufmann, 1977). It is therefore important for scholars (as well as for practical politicians and administrators) to understand how these "street-level bureaucrats" (Lipsky, 1980; Prottas, 1979) actually perform their tasks.

In particular, two forms of treatment should be considered. One might be labeled *bureaucratic,* in this case a pejorative term. The question is the extent to which members of the public bureaucracy use the rules and procedures of their organizations as a means of protecting themselves at the possible expense of the interest of the clients (Sjoberg, Brymer, and Farris, 1978). In the standard model of goal displacement in organizations (Merton, 1940), the goals of self-preservation displace the service goals of the organization. Such may indeed be the case, unfortunately, with the treatment some clients receive from government.

The other way of approaching the treatment of clients by public servants involves to some degree the obverse of bureaucratic behavior, namely the question of the willingness of those in government to attempt to deal humanely and fairly with their clients, especially those from lower-class and minority populations. Do public servants have special obligations of service to these disadvantaged populations? Do such obligations extend beyond the simple application of the rules and regulations?

A number of studies have examined the behavior of administrators and clients, and at least a few have attempted to be comparative. Within the United States, Goodsell (1981) has done extensive research on the interactions of clients and civil servants, and a team at the Institute for Social Research (Katz et al., 1975) has also conducted extensive research from a somewhat different theoretical perspective. Students of "street-level bureaucracy" (Lipsky, 1980; Prottas, 1979) have also examined these relationships, although somewhat more impressionistically and less systematically. In general, the evidence which has been amassed about these interactions is rather positive, despite some of the usual stereotypes of the public servant (Goodsell, 1985). Most citizens report being treated fairly and on the whole quite courteously; the evaluations are in general as good as, and in some cases better than, similar evaluations given of private sector employees.

Although it is now somewhat dated, a major comparative research piece on the relationship between public bureaucrats and their clients appears in the Almond and Verba study *The Civic Culture* (1963:68–78). In particular, citizens in five countries were asked whether they expected fair treatment by the public bureaucracy and the police and whether they expected their views to be taken into consideration by these two bodies. British and American respondents expected the best treatment from their public servants, followed by Germans and then Italians. Mexican respondents by very large percentages did *not* expect fair treatment and consideration from their public ser-

111

vants. Rather similar negative evaluations have been reported about civil servants in other developing countries (Eldersveld, 1965; Eldersveld, Jagannadham, and Barnabas, 1968; Goodsell, 1984; Marinen, 1980). Likewise, limited studies by participant-observers report less favorable treatment of clients (especially lower-status clients) by public servants in some less developed countries than in the more developed countries (see, for example, Goodsell, 1976). Especially interesting interactions occur when public servants from more modernized cultures come into contacts with clients from less developed nations (Katz and Eisenstadt, 1960). To some extent the public servants serve as socializing agents for their clients, but at the same time the particularistic values of the clients require some debureaucratization of the behavior of the public officials if those officials are to be successful in meeting the needs of their new clients. In all these cases, however, the citizen's impression of government may be significantly influenced by interaction with civil servants at the very lowest level in their organizations.

Management. A second aspect of behavior within public organizations is to some extent an extension of the first. This is the relationships between superiors and subordinates within the formal organizational structure. Many attributes, such as the excessive use of rules, and goal displacement, can be observed in the interaction among workers within an organization just as they are observed in relationships between civil servants and their clients. While it may be popular in some circles to examine these interactions from the bottom up and to look at the possibilities of more humane organizations (Argyris, 1964; Frederickson, 1980), here I will adopt more of a managerial stance and will be interested in seeing how organizations can be structured differently in different cultural settings to produce greater compliance by staff within the rules of the organization and greater effectiveness in reaching stated organizational goals. In addition, given the popularity of Japanese-style management (Ouchi, 1981) as a panacea for what ails business (and to a lesser extent for what ails government) in other industrialized countries, we should also question the degree to which managerial styles can effectively be transmitted across cultural boundaries.

Unfortunately, apart from the hymns of praise for Japanese management, relatively little work has been done on comparative management styles and their effectiveness (but see Haire, Ghiselli, and Porter, 1966; Richardson, 1956; Roos and Roos, 1971). The reason may be in part the slowness of students of private sector management to understand the importance of culture in producing effective organizations. Even students of development administration, however, who should have been more sensitive to the influences of cultural and social variables, often simply attempted to transplant Western, hierarchical management structures into situations in which they were almost doomed to fail; this was simply the "modern" way to manage (see Esman, 1966).

The allegation that there have been few comparative studies of management may appear terribly misinformed, given the large number of descriptive studies of public management in country X or public personnel policies in country Y. (The work appearing in the *International Review of Administrative Sciences* is most representative of this genre.) Frequently missing, however, is research which attempts to isolate cultural and social features that may make certain management styles successful in some settings but not in others or research that seeks to compare differences in managerial styles across cultures with some theoretical purpose in mind. The descriptive literature serves as a useful basis for more research of this type, but to date relatively little progress has been made in developing the theoretical perspectives or in understanding the transferability of "administrative science" from one culture to another. What appears to be needed is something on the order of a contingency approach but one built more on social and cultural characteristics than on the characteristics of the production process (Lawrence and Lorsch, 1967).

Implementation. The questions of how members of the public bureaucracy interact with their clients and with the other members of their organization are related to the question of their behavior in the implementation process (Nakamura and

113

Smallwood, 1980; Pressman and Wildavsky, 1973). The word *implementation* has become extremely popular in the study of public administration, although in some ways it merely contains a truth that has been known for some time: things in government do not happen by themselves; someone must make them happen. Implementation research has emphasized the numerous pitfalls which a program may encounter before it goes into effect in the manner intended by those who conceived the program (Hood, 1976). In so doing, however, this research has focused the attention of both scholars and practitioners who want to engage in successful policymaking on the bottom end of the process rather than on questions of adequate policy formulation and design (Linder and Peters, forthcoming).

A good deal of implementation research has been conducted in a number of different political settings (Barrett and Fudge, 1981; Grindle, 1980; Mayntz, 1980). Despite the importance of some of this research, as a model of behavior for the public bureaucracy, however, this research appears to have some serious weaknesses. First, as Bowen (1982) noted quite persuasively, in some ways this approach to behavior in the public bureaucracy is excessively simplistic and mechanistic. It appears to assume that public managers do not have the commitment, or the wit, to engage in complex political stratagems in order to achieve what they want or even more simply what they are supposed to achieve. In the implementation literature, these administrators are presumed to encounter difficulties at one or another clearance points and then roll over and play dead. Bowen draws attention to the number of stratagems in which real-life civil servants and politicians can (and do) engage when they want to achieve something in government.

In addition, the motivational assumptions of the implementation approach to the policy process appear to have been inadequately stated. There seems to be an underlying assumption that many, or most, members of the public bureaucracy will attempt to sabotage policies which are meant to be implemented. This hypothesis is posited with little logical explanation of why they would want to do so or whether they would engage in that destructive behavior even if they wanted to do so. There may well be instances in which new programs and policies are inimical to the interests of established public organizations, and these organizations may well oppose them (Hogwood and Peters, 1985). Much of the implementation literature, however, appears to adopt Allison's (1971) "bureaucratic politics" model without the attention to nuance and to political strategy which that model requires. That is, there appears to be an underlying assumption that the organization is using the decision situation to enhance its own strategic position rather than attempting to achieve the stated objectives of the policy or organization. Hood (1976) quite rightly notes that there will rarely be perfect administration; this statement is, however, quite different from the assumptions of "perverse administration" which appear to lie at the heart of a great deal of the implementation literature.

Corruption. One form of bureaucratic behavior with which most citizens believe they are familiar is corruption. Despite the generally positive evaluations given public administrators in most industrialized countries, there still appears to be a widely held opinion that public servants who are able to do so will engage in questionable practices to increase their own income. In less developed political cultures the belief that there is rampant corruption is pervasive and apparently more frequently justified by the facts. It has been noted any number of times, however, that value systems should not be imposed on the civil service systems of other countries when the indigenous culture accepts what would be considered illegal or corrupt in other societies (for example, Pye, 1962; Quah, 1982). Even in more developed societies, citizens frequently believe that behaviors which may be "maladministration" (Wheare, 1973) or political bargaining are corrupt in a legal sense. The study of corruption is important, however, not only from the value perspective of administrative accountability but also from the practical perspective of understanding how administrative systems actually function.

The difficulty for social scientists in dealing with the question of corrupt behavior by public officials, as with other types of illegal behavior such as tax evasion (Guttman, 1977; Lewis,

1982), is gaining adequate measurements of the behavior's actual occurrence. Some observational measures—typically in instances that Westerners might regard as corrupt but which were widely accepted in another society—have been used. Also, surrogate measures based upon rating scales, or upon administrative overhead, or upon convictions, have been employed for both the American states and Latin America (Correa, 1979, 1985; see also Hoetjes, 1977). These measures provide some interesting insights into bureaucratic behavior but unfortunately may leave as many questions unanswered as answered. The measure used for measuring corruption in the American states, for example—number of convictions of public officials for corrupt behavior—may only partially reflect real levels of corruption. Some states (for example, Louisiana) have long histories and an apparent acceptance of corrupt behavior in public office, so that it may be difficult to obtain convictions even if charges are brought against an official.

Policymaking. The final type of bureaucratic behavior that I will discuss now is the role of the public bureaucracy in making public policy. I will discuss the power of the career civil service vis-à-vis political appointees in some detail in chapter 5 and will not belabor the point here. Here, however, I will mention two very important aspects of the behavior of civil servants as they are engaged in making public policy.

The first is the very basic and important question of how decisions are actually made in government or indeed in any large complex organization. The two major contending models of public decisionmaking have been *incrementalism* and *synopticism* (Braybrooke and Lindblom, 1963; Goodin, 1983; Simon, 1947). Space prohibits a detailed exposition and analysis of these two models, and I will have to oversimplify greatly some of the issues involved. The fundamental question, however, is whether government is capable of making decisions by considering all of its available options (or a large subset) and matching them to its goals or whether government is condemned to make decisions by incremental methods that are tantamount to muddling through. Incremental methods have some compelling logic of their own to justify them but also

116

place governments in the position of reacting to events rather than attempting to anticipate events and potentially to forestall problems (Richardson, 1982). In the United States, it is very easy to conceptualize government as perpetually muddling through, given the generally antigovernment, antiplanning mentality of many observers within and outside government. If government is not very important, or is almost evil, then it is perfectly acceptable to let it muddle through. In other, more etatist political systems, it may be possible to consider more purposive and planned action. In either case, however, we need to distinguish ideologies about policymaking from the manner in which policies are actually made.

The second major question about how policies are made within the public bureaucracy, and by the interaction of that bureaucracy with the remainder of the political system, concerns the relationship with interest groups. We have discussed elsewhere various models of this relationship (Peters, 1984: 150–67) but a great deal of empirical data can be used to examine these patterns of relationships, especially for the Scandinavian countries which have more open and documented involvement of interest groups in government decisionmaking (Fivelsdal, Jørgensen, and Jensen, 1979; Johansen and Kristensen, 1982; Kvavik, 1978). Studies on the behavior of Scandinavian civil servants show behavioral patterns which appear quite different from those expected in other political systems, especially the absence of significant amounts of "turf fighting" when civil servants contend over policy issues. The implication is that the openness of the decisionmaking situation, as well as the content of organizational socialization, contributes to this observed behavior.

Finally, we need to remember that when we speak of decisionmaking and policymaking in public administration, we are talking about a variety of activities. Some of these activities emulate the activities usually thought to occur in the legislature or in the courts. Public bureaucracies make many more rules with the force of law than do legislatures, and they make many more legal decisions than do the courts. Unfortunately, the exercise of these decisionmaking and policymaking activities is analyzed much less frequently than their more strictly administrative functions and then usually from the perspective of administrative law (but see Mashaw, 1983; Stanbury, 1980).

Summary. Thus far I have discussed a number of possible approaches to measuring the behavior of members of the public bureaucracy. Unlike the examination of mass political behavior such as voting, however, such measurement is a difficult task. A great deal of bureaucratic behavior occurs in private and is intended for private consumption only. In addition, to understand the real meaning of occurrences in government may require almost an insider's understanding of the mores and "codes" of those involved. Finally, inasmuch as some of the important political behavior may be, if not illegal, at least suspect, there will be very overt attempts to disguise and hide many actions. Political behavior such as logrolling is by no means illegal, but many citizens regard it as a manifestation of the corruption of those in government. The task confronting the would-be student of bureaucratic behavior is difficult indeed. It is doubly or triply difficult when that attempt extends beyond a single culture.

Utility Maximization in the Public Bureaucracy

Given the difficulties encountered in the direct, empirical analysis of behavior in the public bureaucracy, it is not surprising that many scholars have turned to more idealized models of bureaucratic behavior and have used these models to predict the way in which real-life public officials would and should behave (Breton and Wintrobe, 1975; Niskanen, 1971; Pommerehne and Frey, 1978). The vast majority of these models are based upon economic reasoning, with utility maximization (usually of the head of the organization) the driving factor. As we will note below, many of these models superficially appear valid, but when the underlying assumptions are discussed from a more politicized perspective, and when even limited empirical evidence is mustered, that face validity comes into serious question. It may be that, for better or for worse, the actual behavior of individuals in the public bureaucracy is much more complex than would be predicted by or permitted in most models of their behavior.

The Basic Model

Let us now consider the basic model of bureaucratic behavior as seen from the public choice perspective. Although the graphic presentations and mathematics used to support the reasoning may appear quite complex to some students of public bureaucracy, the underlying logic is actually quite simple. In fact, if anything, it is excessively simple. As I mentioned above, however, the analysis does to some extent appear to agree with the experiences of many scholars and citizens who interact with public bureaucracy and with many other observations of the behavior of public organizations (Downs, 1967; Tullock, 1965).

The goals of public organizations have been classified as being either purposive and related to the achievement of some public purpose or reflexive and related to preserving or enhancing smooth functioning within the organization (Mohr, 1973). The prevailing formalized economic models of bureaucratic behavior stress the reflexive goals of public organizations. These models are based upon the assumption that individuals in public office attempt to maximize their own personal utility (Downs, 1967; Niskanen, 1971) rather than to maximize the delivery of services by their organizations. Rather than stressing self-aggrandizement motives, a few such models (Peacock, 1983) posit the desire on the part of career bureaucrats to have as much "on the job leisure" and as secure a life as possible, and hence an unwillingness to "rock the boat" with aggressive searches for additional funds and policy latitude. This conceptualization, however, may distort and oversimplify reality as much as those that posit an aggressive entrepreneur.

With these basic assumptions, these models of bureaucracy are members of a large class of models of political behavior that reflect rather simplistic economic ideas of utility maximization (Moe, 1984). At the worst these models can become mere tautologies—whatever bureaucrats do must be done to maximize their utility. The more useful models, however, do posit a value or set of values which the bureaucrat will attempt to maximize, and they therefore serve as a basis for empirical testing. While many students of bureaucracy who have spent years in close contact with their subjects reject such seemingly simplistic models out of hand, the internal logic of the approach and the apparent predictive power warrant a more detailed examination.

Apart from our saying that utility is to be maximized, any model of this sort must state a particular quantity which, by being maximized, will maximize the utility of the actor in question. In the case of most of the utility-based models of public bureaucracy, the quantity to be maximized is the size of the agency and its budget. Rational bureaucrats—the "bureau chiefs" in the writings of Niskanen and most others of this school—are assumed to want to maximize the size of their budgets. Why maximize the budget rather than anything else?

The basic logic of this argument is that, by maximizing the size of the bureau, the bureau chief will be able to maximize his or her own personal utility, as measured through salary, perquisites of office, and so forth. This assumption derives from conventional economic theory about the "rent-maximizing" behavior of capitalists and most particularly monopolists (Marris, 1964; Migue and Belanger, 1974). Bureau chiefs in the public sector are further assumed to have much the same latitude to appropriate "profits" for themselves as do managers in private sector firms, so that any extra money in the budget can be translated into personal benefits.

Another logical justification for the maximization of bureau size is discussed less often in this literature but is important nonetheless (but see Downs, 1967). In some analyses the logical justification for budget maximization is more the protection of the organization than the self-aggrandizement of the bureau chief. Public organizations function in a budgetary climate which is uncertain and which is controlled from above—by the "sponsor," in the terms of much of the public choice literature, or more simply by the legislature. It is therefore in the interest of the leadership of a public organization to attempt to maximize the budget in the short run, when possible, and to build in some fat. This fat can be used to protect the organization against future cuts or slow growth. Such budget maximization, however, appears to be better envisioned in a long-term game rather than a short-term game (Wildavsky, 1984:71–79). Short-term gains bought at the expense of a loss of confidence by the sponsors may have negative long-term impacts on the budgetary success of the bureau. In addition to simple budget maximization, a bureau chief may seek to add new functions to his or her bureau. The new functions provide something that future budget cutters can eliminate while still being able to protect the central "heartland" of the organization (Downs, 1967).

This latter conception of the logic of bureaucratic expansion is consistent with the behavior of a bureau chief as much concerned about policy as about personal rewards from office, or it may be simply a conservative strategy to ensure a secure job. The bureau chief may be merely trying to protect the organization so that it offers clients the services that it is currently providing; alternatively, he or she may be trying to reach the twenty or thirty years needed for retirement at full pension with minimal difficulty. The same behavior—budget maximization—may therefore have at least three motivational bases.

Niskanen and others writing from a similar economic perspective have argued that bureaus can be extremely successful in their attempts to maximize their budgets and can logically generate budgets up to twice as large as would be necessary to produce their actual output. The remainder of the resources would be used to augment either the personal life-styles of the administrators in question or to build up fat within the organization's budget as protection against future uncertainties. If this is indeed the case, how can bureaus be so successful when they confront organizations, such as legislatures, which are presumably inhabited by competent and hardheaded individuals?

The basic answer advanced in the literature of economic models of bureaucracy is that the bureaus have a virtual monopoly over information in their policy area, just as the sponsors tend to have a monopoly over money. With this presumed control over information, the bureau is able to present evidence to support its position and perhaps more important is able to hide its true production function for services from the sponsor. The sponsor may then be in the position of trading financial support for limited information that it may be able to use in any subsequent oversight of the bureau. In general, however, the assumption is that the bureau is capable of dominating the sponsor because of the dominance of information. In addition, the output of the bureau is "sold" to the sponsor as a whole for a single budget price in advance of the services that are produced rather than being sold on a per unit basis as they are created. It therefore becomes more difficult for the sponsor adequately to assess the true value of what is being "bought." Assessment is doubly difficult because for many bureaus, for example those administering entitlement programs, it may not be clear exactly how much service will have to be created in the following year.

Another reason why bureaus may be successful, although it is less often modeled in the public choice literature on bureaucracy, is that they have clients, and those clients are voters (Spann, 1977). This more political explanation may be especially powerful in situations where legislative committees rather than the full legislature make the crucial decisions concerning budgetary allocations. In the United States, at least, legislative committees are often composed of representatives with a very strong constituency interest in the policy area about which they make decisions; this is one crucial aspect of the traditional conception of the iron triangle in American politics (Freeman, 1965). The clients of the bureau are therefore also the constituents for the legislator. In such a situation, the legislative committee has little or no incentive to exercise strict oversight over the bureau. On the contrary, the political career of the legislators may well be enhanced by giving the bureau what it demands in the budgetary process, thereby creating benefits for their own constituents. The legislators can then claim credit for the benefits (Mayhew, 1974).

The Logical Critique

I have now briefly explained the basic arguments of the Niskanen (and related) models of public bureaucracy. Thus far I have offered little comment, but I will now critique the approach before presenting some limited empirical evidence which seems to call into question some or all of the basic assumptions of the model. A detailed logical critique of the model has already been presented in several places (Goodin, 1982; Jackson, 1982; Kogan, 1973), but some of the points bear repeating, and additional points can be made. This critique is not just an exercise in condemning scholars who bring models and assumptions from other disciplines into the study of political science and public administration. Rather, it is recognition that these models are important as a starting point for a more political and more empirical examination of behavior of public administrators. At the very least, these models have as a virtue that they clearly state their assumptions and follow their analysis through to its logical conclusion rather than engaging in the vacillation and equivocation characteristic of many less formal presentations.

The first, and perhaps most basic, question about the formal models of bureaucratic behavior is the assumption that bureau chiefs engage in maximizing behavior. The assumption that individuals or organizations can maximize values in complex decisionmaking situations, which dates back at least to Simon's (1947) analysis of "administrative man," has been extremely suspect and is probably especially so for public organizations, which by their nature have quite complex relationships with their environment and with other components of the public sector.

123

The highly rationalistic conception of organizational behavior in the economic models conflicts with many other conceptions, based more upon sociological and political reasoning, that suggest the irrationality of most large, complex organizations. Although two of his three perspectives on decisionmaking imply rationality, for example, Allison's (1971) analysis of the Cuban missile crisis also discusses an "organizational behavior" model that stresses many of the irrationalities of large-scale organizations. This model was set in a policy area which may allow for somewhat clearer goals than would be true for most domestic policies. Cohen, March, and Olsen (1972) describe organizational decisionmaking as a "garbage can" in which means and ends, facts and values, and decisions and justifications are all mixed together. A strictly ordered series of preferences and rational, maximizing behavior has little place in such a seemingly irrational world. Even some scholars who have analyzed the activities of private sector firms (Cyert and March, 1963) see the firm's behavior as much less maximizing than neoclassical economics might suggest. Instead, firms seek solutions which produce acceptable, but not maximum, profits. Those writers who argue for organizational rationality may well be correct, but they must refute a great deal of evidence and analysis stressing quite contrary views.

Associated with the problem of maximization is the problem of a certain brand of methodological individualism. The models appear to assume that the bureau chief is functioning alone and autonomously and is capable of making whatever decisions he or she wishes. In the real world of public organizations, however, the bureau chief is functioning in a highly complex and politicized world in which decisions involve negotiation and compromise as much as they do the imposition of the values of a single individual. We must therefore attempt to understand the organizational and institutional framework from which decisions emerge if we want to be able to understand and predict decisions.

If we assume for the time being that bureau chiefs could indeed maximize, what would they choose to maximize? Economic models of bureaucracy clearly imply that they would maximize the size of their organizations' budgets. This notion corresponds quite closely to one popular view of the public bureaucracy as a group of aggressive, self-aggrandizing entrepreneurs participating in the political process primarily from self-interest. There are, however, at least three other possible motivations for any attempts at maximizing behavior on the part of the bureau chiefs and other bureaucrats in government.

One possible motivation would be that these public officials would prefer an easy, quiet, and safe career to an exciting, rewarding career with a maximum budget. This image of the bureaucrat accords with another popular belief, that the typical bureaucrat is rather lazy, risk averse, and concerned with protecting a retirement pension. Peacock (1979, 1983), in fact, uses many of the same economic tools of Niskanen and others who posit budget maximization to develop a model which maximizes bureaucrats' quiet life and on-the-job leisure rather than maximizing budgets. He further calls attention to the extremely different problems of accountability and control which that approach (as opposed to budget maximization) raises. Certainly, this is as plausible an approach (albeit still with the problem of maximization) as the budget-maximizing approach.

Another manner in which the "rational" bureaucrat may seek to maximize his or her career is by seeking positions in small, elite organizations, or even by *cutting* the size of budgets rather than increasing them. In the United Kingdom, for example, the Treasury is a rather small organization—some 2,300 employees in a total white-collar civil service of almost 600,000 (Council of Civil Service Unions, April 1986). Yet few civil servants would not regard some time spent in the Treasury as enhancing their career, and the first permanent secretary in Treasury is one of the two most powerful civil servants in the country. For many civil servants the power and control exercised by their organization may be more important than mere size (Kogan, 1973). Even in the United States, for which the Niskanen model was intended, some public officials (for example, James Schlesinger) have made a mark by reducing the size of their organizations rather than increasing it (Breton and Wintrobe, 1975:205). In fairness, however, one career pattern which could lead to budget maximization would be that of attempting to maximize one's personal rewards in subsequent positions (perhaps in the private sector in the United States) by budgetary success in the present position (Tullock, 1974).

Finally, people in government might possibly attempt to maximize the stated service goals of their bureaus or might indeed be concerned about something called the public interest. Government and its civil servants will find this a difficult position to accept, but some of the available empirical evidence (for example, that marshaled in Goodsell, 1985) would indicate that many in public office are attempting to do a good job and to provide needed services. Paradoxically, many who are attempting to do a good job feel that they are hampered in doing so by the numerous laws and regulations that control their behavior. These regulations reflect the assumption that they would rather maximize their own rewards or their own leisure in office than act in the public interest. The slow and cumbersome behavior of public bureaucracies may therefore have become a self-fulfilling hypothesis.

If we now suspend our incredulity and assume that indeed bureau chiefs do attempt to maximize, and that what they attempt to maximize is the size of their bureaus' budgets, can they really extract any personal advantage from this activity? In the majority of political systems it would seem to be difficult to extract anything other than a few perquisites of office, and consequently most bureau chiefs would have little to gain for themselves from aggressive attempts to maximize their budgets.

In most political systems the salaries for most civil servants, and indeed for most political executives, are established by law. Likewise, in a large number of governments, even the perquisites available to a bureau chief—the quality of the furniture, the presence and thickness of carpeting, and so on—are also determined centrally. Given that the majority of bureau chiefs are at or near the top of the civil service ladder, they can gain very little materially from the work required to maximize a budget and to manage it once it has been obtained. Some things, such as the number of executive secretaries and the ranking and quality of staff, may depend upon the size of the organization, but these benefits—and things such as bragging rights on the cocktail party circuit—are much more the intangible psychological benefits of budgetary "success" than those discussed by the economic theorists. In some ways, an expansion in the budget would principally benefit not the bureau chiefs but the employees beneath the chief who may expect promotion and perhaps additional perquisites (Stahl, 1976). In fairness it must be said that some reformulations of the basic model have received empirical support. They depend upon maximizing labor input into the production of public services (Orzechowski, 1977; Spann, 1977), on the assumption that bureaucrats either simply like larger staffs or want to create more bureaucrat-voters to generate larger budgets in the future. This empirical support, however, reflects local government organizations with service provision functions rather than white-collar organizations such as those that one would encounter at the center of a national government. Even there, however, would all the political and administrative work be justified by these relatively meager benefits for the bureau chief?

Finally, we must ask whether the legislative "sponsors" of these bureaucratic organizations are really as inept and unsophisticated as the literature would have us believe. In order for these formal models to work effectively, the sponsor must not be able to monitor the behavior of the bureaus adequately. While it is extremely difficult to ascertain the production functions for most bureaucratic organizations (including those in the private sector; Blankart, 1980), the legislative bodies supplying funds to the bureaucracy can nevertheless exercise oversight over their activities.

Budgetary committees and substantive policy committees, at least in the United States, appear to have little trouble in assessing the relative efficiency of organizations under their purview. These evaluations may not be formal economic assessments of the organizations' production functions, but they still offer a good starting point for discussion of budget requests. Even if the committees are wrong in their initial assessments, the appropriations process is sufficiently detailed to permit the gathering of information to develop a more accurate picture. Also, much of the anecdotal evidence about the behavior of budget committees suggests their tendency to concentrate attention on the very types of things which our bureau chiefs are presumed to want to maximize—salaries, new secretaries and staff, and so on—rather than broad policy issues. Furthermore, the budgetary process is a historical process and is carried on by many of the same actors year after year. A bureau may be able to fool a committee in the short run but would find it extremely difficult to do so in the long run. In addition, the individual members of the committee develop their own expertise over time and become more capable of developing their own policy information.

Then, too, there is not the dearth of information about public policy issues which these models assume. First, there has been the development of institutions such as the Congressional Budget Office, and the staffs of committees in Congress have increased. These provide the research needed for the legislature to make more informed decisions about appropriations and the performance of bureaus, particularly with the increasing capability of the General Accounting Office (Mosher, 1979) to evaluate bureaucratic performance. Finally, a large number of interest groups, consulting firms, and other sources of information outside government are more than willing to offer Congress all the information it needs. Some or most of the information will be biased, but the "issue networks" (Heclo, 1978) that form around policy issues do not allow the bureaus to monopolize the supply of information.

Even in countries without such well-developed legislative institutions, other institutions of government appear to have little difficulty in evaluating the performance of government organizations and in making budgetary allocations based upon that assessment. The Treasury in the United Kingdom, for example, appears to know rather well what ministries and their component parts are doing and can develop well-informed judgments about their budgetary needs (Ashford, 1981; Heclo

128

and Wildavsky, 1974). In other countries, the Ministry of Finance will perform a rather similar budgetary function (Lord, 1973). Also, improved (or at least different) budgeting procedures have begun to place a greater emphasis on the per unit costs of services being produced so that the lump-sum "sale" of services may no longer be totally accurate. In short, it is simply not as easy to try to fool the budgetary sponsors of bureaus as we are sometimes led to believe.

The formal models of bureaucratic behavior tend to posit somewhat unrealistic goals for Congress. The assumption appears to be that congressmen do indeed want to make good public policy and are willing to trade money for information. We should not denigrate Congress too readily, but many writers (for example, Fiorina, 1977; Mayhew, 1974) have noted that congressmen may have a stronger incentive to ensure their own reelection than to do anything else. If so, then they have more incentives to please their constituents than to please bureaucrats, and one way of pleasing many constituencies— leaving aside the residents of Northern Virginia and Prince George's and Montgomery counties in Maryland—is to keep civil service pay low. Congressmen can also score political points by visibly exercising oversight over the bureaucracy. By this recipe Congress would not abdicate power to bureau chiefs but rather wrest power from them. In general, these economic models appear to have presented rather unrealistic views of the abilities, behavior, and motivations of the "sponsors" in the legislature.

Even before beginning to consider some limited data regarding the behavior of bureau chiefs, I have formulated a number of questions about the logic of approaches which posit single-minded, rational behavior for public officials. Their world appears too complex, and their own motivations too mixed, ever to conform to such a monomaniacal behavior pattern. Even if officials were motivated in the way that these models suggest, civil service regulations and other government rules leave relatively little room for personal gain from success in office. Finally, institutions which support the bureaus in government do not appear nearly as inadequate and ill informed as might be supposed. We can therefore approach our empirical analysis with a good deal of skepticism.

The Empirical Analysis of Bureaucratic Behavior: The Economic Model

Let us now consider the apparent behavior of public bureaucrats or at least the manifestations of that behavior through public budget and personnel decisions. My empirical analysis will attempt to determine how closely the Niskanen model fits the reality of occurrences in several national governments. We will, of course, have to infer any motivations for the behavior of bureau chiefs (and others) in question from the observed patterns of data. As noted above, any one observed behavior of a bureau chief may be interpreted in at least three ways. Thus there may be some divergence between the *act meaning* of some behaviors (the interpretation which the researcher imposes) and the *action meaning* (the meaning attached by the actors themselves). This difficulty is inherent when we try to make inferences about behavior from aggregate data (Harmon, 1981; Pollitt, 1984), but (as in this instance) there may be no other way of approaching an important research topic.

Although the Niskanen family of models has been widely used in explaining bureaucratic behavior, there has been relatively little empirical examination of the models' predictive capabilities (but see Spann, 1977). The reason may be that scholars with an interest in formal models tend to have relatively little interest in the empirical testing of the models or because those with a more detailed knowledge of the underlying realities about the public bureaucracy have dismissed the formal models out of hand for the logical reasons that I mentioned above. For whatever reason, there appears to be a need for very detailed empirical examination of the models.

One attempt to examine the models' predictions directly comes from the United Kingdom. Hood, Huby, and Dunsire (1984) examined the implications of the model in British central administration and developed several hypotheses concerning developments in the United Kingdom during the period 1971 to 1982 (when the public budget was increasing rapidly) that could be expected to occur if the model was correct. First, they hypothesized that public sector pay would increase as fast as or faster than total public expenditure if civil servants were able to appropriate budgetary increases for their own benefit. Second, they hypothesized that the pay for senior officials would increase more rapidly than pay for lower grades if the bureau chiefs and their immediate associates were able to glean personal benefits from budgetary expansion. Third, they hypothesized that civil service staff should increase more rapidly than the budget if the assumptions about the preference for labor over other inputs (Orzechowski, 1977) were valid. Finally, they hypothesized that there would be an increase in the number of chiefs relative to the number of Indians if bureau heads were in fact using budgetary increases to expand their own staffs.

There was relatively little or no support for most of these hypotheses in the United Kingdom. In some ministries the latter two hypotheses did receive some support, but it was not possible to predict which ministries would fit the pattern and which would not. Ministries concerned with local government and territorial issues (the Department of the Environment, the Scottish Office, and the Welsh Office), however, did demonstrate a personnel pattern more akin to that predicted by the economic models than the other ministries, although the reason is not apparent, unless these ministries needed more extensive field staffs. The three authors conclude their article with an expression of the need to specify more fully the content of the economic models and the conditions under which they may be expected to be successful in predicting bureaucratic behavior.

We should not be surprised if these economic models are not particularly successful in the United Kingdom. After all, the models were developed largely with reference to the United States, which has a much more decentralized public bureaucracy than the United Kingdom. In the United States, we would expect bureau chiefs to be able to operate more as autonomous entrepreneurs, while those in the United Kingdom operate within the context of a unified civil service with tight fiscal and personnel controls exercised by the Treasury and by the ministries. Even the idea of the bureau has relatively little meaning in the United Kingdom. Hood, Huby, and Dunsire (1984) had to analyze whole ministries rather than smaller bureaus and agencies (see also Hood and Dunsire, 1981). It is therefore important to attempt to apply some of the same measures to developments in the U.S. federal bureaucracy and determine how closely these conform to those found in the United Kingdom. Everything else being equal, we would expect the United States to resemble the economists' world of bureaucracy more than did the United Kingdom.

In an analysis of survey data of state administrators in the United States, Sigelman (1986) found very little evidence to support an assumption of budget-maximizing behavior by bureaucrats. Only about a third of the respondents were pressing for large budget increases each year, and large numbers said that they wanted no budget increases for the upcoming year. Furthermore, the general commitment of the respondents to government programs, rather than being necessarily a commitment to their own individual program goals or its growth, was most important in explaining the desire to expand the agency's budget. It appears that some bureau chiefs simply perceive that government can create good things for the society more than do others, and that is related to their desire to spend more money.

Given that we are not interviewing the bureau chiefs whose actions we are observing, we have no way of knowing whether they have in fact been attempting to maximize their budgets. We can therefore only look at the success or failure of those actors in getting what they are presumed to want from the policymaking process. If, however, the predicted pattern of increasing budgets does not appear, and benefits of a more personal nature do not increase in particular, then the economic models are in some difficulty. Either the motivations of the bureau chiefs were not as posited or the political process does not permit them to play the type of aggressive game or role that was assumed. In either case, the public bureaucracy would not be the Leviathan which it is presumed to be by people writing from the economic perspective.

The rather unusual structure of the executive branch in the United States, compared with that in most other industrialized countries, raises some interesting questions relating to measurement and to the interpretation of these models. The most fundamental question is: who are the bureau chiefs? It is unclear whether we are talking about the upper echelons of the career civil service or the political executives in Washington for short-term assignments (Heclo, 1977). While the former may have more incentives to feather their own nest—since they expect to be in government for an entire career—they may be less able to do so. Also, the relative positions of the two sets of actors have been changing over the past several decades and especially during the Reagan administration: the number of careerists who are bureau chiefs has been decreasing. Careerists' abilities to bring about any budgetary changes to benefit themselves is thus also likely to have decreased, especially in the early 1980s, when some political appointees are committed conservatives who would want to decrease the amount of government spending and perhaps especially spending for the civil service.

Hood, Huby, and Dunsire (1984) first addressed the relative position of the civil service at a macro level to see whether the pay and perquisites for civil servants as a group kept increasing during the decade in question. This was a decade of significant expansion in public expenditure, and there should have been enough expansion in the resource base for use by aggressive managers who wanted to expand their fiefdoms. Likewise, in the United States, we will consider the increases in federal white-collar civil service pay in the period 1970 to 1984 and will compare these to other movements in the economy such as economic growth, inflation, and increases in the compensation of employees in all industries. As in the United Kingdom, this was a time of great expansion in the public sector, so that "free-floating resources" would have been around for the ag-

Table 16. Cumulative Changes in Civil Service Pay
Rates and Economic Indicators, 1971–1984

Retail price index	Gross national product[a]	Personal income[a]	Total federal expenditure	Civil service pay
167.8	230.3	235.7	240.8	113.0[b]

[a]Current dollars.
[b]Based on annual raises awarded by president and Congress but not taking into account promotions, step increases, and so on.
Sources: U.S. Bureau of the Census (annual-b, annual-a).

gressive bureaucratic entrepreneur to appropriate. These findings are reported in table 16.

It is rather clear from the evidence in table 16 that the civil service has not been successful in protecting its economic position as a service during the past decade and a half. Civil service pay has increased less than half as fast as total personal income in the United States and has declined significantly as a portion of total federal expenditure. Rather than being labor intensive, federal spending has become "transfer intensive." There have been large increases in spending in programs (for example, Social Security) that require relatively few employees per dollar spent. In addition, civil service pay has not even kept pace with inflation and appears to have fallen approximately one-third behind the rate of increases in prices. To judge from its performance, this is not an institution which wants to maximize its own income and finds it relatively easy to do so. In fact, the failure of the "sponsors"—both Congress and the President—to supply pay increases is reflected in the relatively poor economic position of federal employees. The Pay Act of 1970 provided for elaborate machinery for guaranteeing the comparability of public sector pay. In more years than not, however, the president has recommended pay increases below the level recommended to maintain comparability, and these have been approved by Congress (Peters, 1985b). The sponsors apparently pay a good deal more attention to the political mileage to be gained by offering lower salaries to federal employees than they do to the power of the civil service within the policymaking process and its presumed monopoly of information.

Table 17. Changes in Salary Levels, 1970–1984, by Grade (percent)

Executive level II	G.S. 18[a]	G.S. 12	G.S. 8	G.S. 2
+133	+140	+141	+138	+123

[a]And top SES grade; does not include possibility of performance bonuses.
Source: Office of Management and Budget (annual-a).

Given that the formal analyses of public bureaucracy have focused largely on the bureau chief, we must also consider the *relative* changes in compensation of different groups of civil servants. Again, we should take into account not only the top levels of the career staff and their salaries but also the political appointees who, in 1986, are more likely to be bureau chiefs. As table 17 shows, there is relatively little difference in the increases in salaries (rates of change are for the top of each salary grade), and at least the salaries for Executive Level II positions have fared slightly less well than those for other grades. It would not appear from these data that bureau chiefs have been able to feather their own nests at the expense of the taxpayers or indeed at the expense of other civil servants. This situation is similar to that in the United Kingdom, where top positions in the civil service fared substantially worse than the civil service as a whole in the period researched by Hood, Huby, and Dunsire. In the mid-1980s, however, the top grades have been able to pull ahead in some years because their salaries are reviewed by a separate body (Top Salaries Review Body), and the top grades have not been subject to the same controls as other civil servants (*FDA News*, July/August, 1985).

Salary levels in the civil service may, however, be only a part of the compensation picture in Washington. One of the standard complaints about the political power of the civil service is that civil servants have been able to enhance the perquisites of their office, not least of which are inflation-proofed pensions. This was one of the major criticisms of the civil service system offered by the Grace Commission (President's Private Sector Survey on Cost Control, 1984), and it is a part of the conventional wisdom about the Washington bureaucracy. The same complaints have been made in any number of other political systems.

Table 18. Changes in Components of Total Compensation, 1970–1984

Component	Percentage change
Total	+144
Direct compensation	+118
Personnel benefits	+456

Source: Office of Management and Budget (annual-b).

The data in table 18 compare changes in *total compensation* for federal civil servants with similar changes in the entire economy. These data demonstrate that, while direct compensation for federal employees has indeed grown quite sluggishly, the employee benefits offered have increased significantly. This development in part reflects the rapidly increasing costs of inflation-proofed pensions during an extremely inflationary time (just to keep up with inflation, pensions would need to increase by 168 percent), as well as the increasing number of employees eligible to retire. In 1970 fewer than 1 million people were receiving federal retirement benefits, but by 1984 the number had more than tripled, reaching 3.5 million. Finally, another major component of personnel benefit costs—health care costs—had increased significantly faster than the rate of inflation (208 percent versus 167 percent). When these factors are taken into account, the expansion of personnel benefit expenditures does not appear quite so dramatic, although there has certainly been an increase.

A second measure of the success of the civil service as an

institution in budgetary politics is its ability to expand in numbers and more particularly its ability to add personnel in upper-
echelon positions. As I noted above, some scholars have argued
that the budget-maximizing bureau chief should prefer adding
labor rather than capital. Furthermore, additional personal
staff is one of the few real benefits that a bureau chief may be
able to appropriate, given rather uniform pay and perquisites in
the civil service.

Table 19. Federal Civilian Employment, 1950–1984

Year	Number	Percentage of Labor Force
1950	1,934,040	3.1
1955	2,371,462	3.6
1960	2,370,826	3.4
1965	2,496,064	3.4
1970	2,884,307	3.5
1975	2,848,014	3.1
1980	3,065,672	2.9
1981	2,891,844	2.7
1982	2,860,754	2.6
1983	2,863,071	2.6
1984	2,901,137	2.6

Source: U.S. Bureau of the Census (annual-b).

As table 19 shows, the total federal civil service has not been
expanding rapidly in absolute numbers in the past decade, after
significant increases in the 1960s and 1970s. It has certainly
not been expanding as a proportion of the total labor force in
the United States (see also Peters, 1985b) and has been declining steadily for the past several years—even before the Reagan
administration. Again, this trend does not suggest an institution capable of protecting and expanding its own interests. In
the face of what is apparently substantial political opposition,
it has been losing its position in the economy, both in terms of
the salaries being offered and the numbers of people being employed.

Sheer numbers of civil servants, however, may not be a sufficient measure of the behavior of the budget-maximizing bureau chiefs in enhancing their own positions in public sector employment. One possible measure raised by Hood, Huby, and Dunsire (1984) is the ratio of chiefs to Indians, or the ratio of the number of senior positions relative to lower-level positions in civil service. As table 20 shows, however, the percentages of employees in different grades within the career civil service has remained relatively stable over the fourteen years in question. In particular, the proportion of very top civil servants (G.S. 16 and above) has not increased. If we add executive-level appointments (not in the General Schedule), the proportion of "chiefs" increases slightly, but only slightly, over this period. This relative stability has occurred during a period in which information processing and other technological advances might have been expected to reduce the number of openings for lower-level employees and in which the increasing professional and technical thrust of the federal government might have been expected to require more highly skilled, and highly ranked, personnel.

Elsewhere in their discussion of chiefs and Indians, Hood, Huby, and Dunsire stated that the hiring of additional personal secretaries (a very important perquisite in the British civil service) to assist the "chiefs" indicates bureaucratic power. It is difficult to obtain comparable information for secretarial and clerical positions in the United States, but one surrogate mea-

Table 20. Federal Civil Service by Grade, 1970 and 1984 (percent)

Grade	1970	1984
G.S. 1–6	41.3	36.3
G.S. 7–10	24.0	24.1
G.S. 11–12	21.0	24.3
G.S. 13–15	13.0	14.7
G.S. 16+	0.7	0.6

Source: Office of Personnel Management (biennial).

sure could be the grading of the total secretarial staff in General Schedule employment. We will assume that secretaries who were given posts as executive or personal secretaries would receive higher rankings than would the remainder of those employed in the same personnel category of "secretary." When we examine the civil service gradings across time (Office of Personnel Management, biennial), however, we find that over this decade and a half the average gradings of secretaries have declined slightly, and the number of very highly graded secretaries (at G.S. 12 and above) has been reduced to virtually zero. If this surrogate measure has any validity at all, then there is additional evidence that either bureaucratic entrepreneurs do not want to maximize the size of their budgets and personal staffs or, if they want to do so, they are not terribly successful.

Another means of looking at the ability of budget maximizers to appropriate benefits for themselves is to examine the development of staff positions in the public bureaucracy and particularly personal staffs for the top executives. At this point we shift from figures which are aggregated across the entire civil service to more micro-level data within individual public organizations. Few data sources are sufficiently detailed to permit us to examine the immediate personal staffs of administrators, but it is possible to consider the size of the offices which serve the top executives in departments and other large organizations and also the composition of those offices. In particular, I will examine the changing composition of the offices of eight cabinet secretaries in departments which did not undergo major reorganizations from 1970 to 1984 and the administrators of the General Services Administration and National Aeronautics and Space Administration during the same time period used for my examination of other changes in the bureaucracy. The departments included are Agriculture, Commerce, Interior, Justice, Labor, State, Transportation, and Treasury. Defense was not included because of the presentation of personnel in the 1970 *Budget* along program budgeting lines and the impossibility of distinguishing all employees in the Office of the Secretary of Defense or in the offices of the secretaries of the several armed services. The Department of

Table 21. Changes in Offices of Chief Administrators, Cabinet Departments, and Large Agencies, 1970–1984

Office	Percentage change
Total department	+30
Office of Chief Administrators	+81
G.S. 13+	+157
G.S. 15+	+138

Source: Office of Management and Budget (annual-a).

Housing and Urban Development did not differentiate personnel by office or program in the 1970 *Budget.*

The data on these offices (table 21) provide much greater support than any of the previous data for the posited maximizing behavior of bureau chiefs. In these ten organizations the office of the chief executive increased more than twice as fast as employment in the entire department. The proportion of the members of these offices at high civil service levels increased even more rapidly. While some of the changes observed may represent new tasks being added to the office of the chief executive (for example, greater concern about equal opportunity employment), there is some apparent building of larger personal staffs for these executives. Whether these political appointees—and indeed major political appointees—who have within their own organizations large numbers of bureaus can really be construed to be the "bureau chiefs" discussed in the literature is an important question, but here we do find some limited evidence of bureaucratic expansion.

Finally, we should disaggregate the public bureaucracy even farther and examine the behavior of those organizations which appear to be successful and those which appear to be less successful in the budgetary process. In particular, we have examined the fifteen federal agencies which were most successful in the budgetary process and the fifteen which were least successful in increasing their appropriations over the period 1970–1984. We wanted to know whether those who were seemingly capable of getting more appropriations for their programs also added personnel at differentially high rates and whether they tended to add more highly ranked "chiefs." Likewise, we wanted to see whether those with little success in the budgetary arena behaved differently, and if so, how.

The first major finding of this exercise is that for the rapidly growing agencies staffing levels did not on average increase at the same rate as they did on budgetary levels. The reason is in part that these agencies were in many cases agencies which are transfer rather than labor intensive (for example, Federal Crop Insurance Corporation and the Urban Mass Transit Administration). In general, however, there was not nearly as large an increase in personnel as in spending, with personnel increasing less than one-quarter as fast as expenditures on average within the fifteen fastest-growing agencies. In addition, there was no significant correlation ($r = .08$) between how rapidly an organization's budget increased and how rapidly its personnel levels increased. In fact, two of the rapidly growing organizations actually had declining personnel numbers over the period.

There was somewhat more correlation between the expenditure and personnel numbers for the slowest-growing organizations, but even here the relationship was far from overwhelming ($r = .19$). Some of the slow-growing organizations lost up to one-half of their total employees, while others that grew no faster almost doubled their number of employees. These data appear to indicate that a wide range of factors may affect the behavior of bureau chiefs and their political sponsors in deciding how much to spend, how to spend, and how many people to hire. There is little consistent support for the simple employment-maximizing model of the public bureaucracy among these white-collar organizations.

I have now tested the predictions arising from the Niskanen (1971) and similar economic models of public bureaucracy as much as possible. As I noted above, we cannot test the underlying assumption of the budget-maximizing motivations of the bureaucrats, but I have been able to test some of the predictions about the success of the public bureaucracy in feathering its own nest at the expense of the public and the bureaucrats' preference for employment when there is any "surplus" in the appropriations granted to them. The data that we have been able to muster for the United States offer almost no support for the predictive validity of these models. This was also true for the data for the United Kingdom presented by Hood, Huby, and Dunsire (1984). The results for the United States are especially damning, given that the models were developed with the decentralized and entrepreneurial nature of American government in mind. Therefore, despite their appeal and their specificity, these models seem to have little to recommend them as models of the real world of public bureaucracy.

Conclusion

It is difficult to conduct research on the behavior of public employees directly. Much of the important activity occurs in private, and information may be accessible to the researcher only after the passage of months or even years. That information may be available only from participants who have an interest in certain interpretations of the facts. In addition, a great deal of the behavior of senior civil servants at the decision-making level occurs in an environment which is well understood by the participants but which may be difficult for outsiders to understand adequately. Communication takes place as much in the "code" of the mandarin class as in plain language. Such difficulties are, of course, accentuated when directly comparative research is the goal. Such research has certainly been done, and done successfully, but it is extremely difficult.

This chapter has examined a way of approaching the behavior of members of the public bureaucracy indirectly. Beginning with an important model of bureaucratic behavior, we have asked how closely indicators of behavior available in the public domain correspond to the model. The answer was "not very well." This exercise sought not to debunk models, especially models imported from economics that purport to explain the behavior of public officials, but rather to understand an important facet of the behavior of public bureaucrats using available information and to demonstrate the importance of building clear and explicit models of bureaucratic behavior that can help us examine behavior systematically and comparatively. We already knew that the model did not work in the United Kingdom, but the research reported here demonstrates its weaknesses even in the United States, where it was developed. This type of exercise can, however, help us build systematic knowledge about public bureaucracy. Now at least we know that one model that is plausible (at least in part) has little empirical verification, and we can proceed to develop more and better representations of administrative behavior in the public sector.

5

The Pursuit
of
Power

> Yes, I do think there is a real dilemma here, in that while it has
> been government policy to regard policy as the responsibility of
> Ministers and administration as the responsibility of officials,
> questions of administrative policy can cause confusion between
> the administration of policy and the policy of administration,
> especially when the responsibility for the administration of the
> policy of administration conflicts or overlaps with respon-
> sibility for the policy of the administration of policy.
>
> J. Lynn and A. Jay, *Yes, Minister*

The last of the four possible dependent variables in the study of
public bureaucracies is power. Power is certainly a classic concern of the social sciences, ranging from the sociology of com-
munities to international relations (Dahl, 1957; Hunter, 1953;
Lasswell and Kaplan, 1950; Morgenthau, 1948). It is also a
crucial concept in the comparative study of government and
public administration (Ham and Hill, 1984; Long, 1962). In particular, we are concerned with how policy is actually made in
government and with the role which the public bureaucracy
plays in this process. Therefore, in this chapter we will shift
our attention toward the very upper reaches of government,
where political officials—ministers and their appointees—interact with their very senior career officials in making policy
decisions. The shift means not that I have forgotten my earlier
admonition about the power of field staffs in determining policy in practice but only that we must also be very much concerned with the initial design of policies (Linder and Peters,
1985). The upper echelons of government have been examined
very frequently, although at times the power relations have
been more assumed than determined to exist. In this chapter,

therefore, I will pose a set of questions, without always providing definitive answers, about the relationship of politicians and bureaucrats as they make public policy.

Power, an undeniably important component in the study of the public bureaucracy, is an extremely difficult concept to measure, especially within the secretive and highly nuanced world of the upper echelons of government. Power may be being exercised, but it is being exercised so quietly and indeed so efficiently that it will be difficult to discern, from the day-to-day operations of a smoothly oiled government organization, who actually wields the power. In fact, it may be most difficult to locate power in those political systems where the norms about the locus and exercise of power are the clearest. Also, there may be elaborate dances to allow those in formal position of power to believe—or at least to be seen as believing—that they are actually in charge, while in reality others may in effect govern.

The difficulty of identifying and measuring power directly in the relationship between civil servants and their nominal political masters presents an interesting and difficult research question. One means of approaching this difficult question is to develop ideal-type models of the interactions of the actors to use in determining how closely reality conforms to the ideal. This is, of course, the manner in which Weber sought to identify the characteristics of the perfect bureaucracy, although no structure conforming perfectly to the model has perhaps ever existed (Page, 1985; Udy, 1959). The evidence which can be brought to bear on my research question is largely anecdotal but valuable nonetheless. The development of the ideal types will provide a means of organizing and interpreting the "data" so that we may begin to answer the important question that has been raised.

The Nature of the Problem

One of the most crucial arenas of institutional politics in contemporary industrialized democracies is the interaction of political executives and career civil servants. The interactions of these individuals are crucial in enabling government to perform its routine tasks and to make and implement the decisions required of a modern political system. These interactions are also important for the functioning of an effective political democracy. Political executives, either elected directly by the people or appointed by elected representatives, are presumed to carry with them a mandate to enact and implement the policies they advocated during their electoral campaigns. These political executives, however, are constantly reporting that they believe themselves to be thwarted in their policymaking efforts by the power of an entrenched public bureaucracy. Some of their frustration may be the product of unreasonable expectations that they held prior to entering office, but some may be real.

The roadblocks actually presented by the bureaucracy are most commonly not placed there because of a desire to sabotage one or another set of political leaders for partisan reasons. Rather the obstacles arise from the tendency of large organizations to proceed from inertia along established routes and to persist in doing so until they are stopped; in addition, the bureaucrats and their organizations tend to believe sincerely that they understand the policy area in question better than the political executive, who may be in office for only a short time (Goodsell, 1985). For whatever reasons, however, many ministers or cabinet secretaries believe themselves to be hampered in producing the policies they desire.

If the perceptions of these political executives are accurate, two types of efforts are needed. One is an analytic effort to develop a better conceptual understanding of the politics across and within the real and perceptual gulf separating the two sets of actors. The second is the more normatively driven problem of designing institutional arrangements which will allow bureaucracies to be energized by political leaders while still preserving the permanence, expertise, and partisan (if not policy) impartiality of the public bureaucracy (Doig, 1983; Peters, 1986a).

Two fundamental points should be made at the outset. First, the paragraphs above appear to resurrect and to enshrine the relics of the (with luck) long-dead dichotomy between politics and administration (Campbell and Peters, 1988; Doig, 1983). To some extent, they do indeed do so but to some extent they do not. On the one hand we are recognizing quite explicitly that administration is not merely the execution of policies decided upon by political officials; this point is quite central to the entire concern of the exercise. Administrative officials are indeed deeply involved in policymaking and fight for their own positions and for their own conceptions of "good" policies. On the other hand, however, although they are both engaged in policymaking, political and administrative leaders play very different roles in the policy process.

Career civil servants, by virtue of their permanence, longer time perspective, and functional expertise, take a different view of policy and policymaking from that held by the political executive. The political executive in most governments is only in office for a short period of time and must accomplish something in that time—if only so that he or she can hold another office sometime in the future. Political executives therefore cannot afford to advocate policies which take a long time to come to fruition although they may be technically superior (Murphy, Nuechterlein, and Stupak, 1978). Also, the identification of a career civil servant with a single department or agency (especially in the United States, although this statement is true in most other systems after some point in an individual's career) may make the civil servant's perceptions of desirable policies quite different from the politician's. Finally, the politics of the career civil servant are organizationally based rather than partisan. He or she is engaged in politics to protect or promote an organization (although not necessarily for the reasons discussed in chapter 4) and the values which it embodies rather than to promote a political party or political career.

The conflicts which may exist among civil servants and their political masters have produced a number of attempts on the part of politicians, even in countries lacking such a tradition, to politicize the civil service and make partisan loyalty more of a criterion for appointment and advancement (Meyers, 1985; Ståhlberg, 1985), especially in the case of appointment to very

147

senior positions. As I will note throughout this chapter, this stress on partisan loyalty has been a very fundamental change for countries such as the United Kingdom, which have a tradition of an extremely impartial civil service but increasingly feel the need for a more ideologically committed civil service (Institute of Directors, 1986; Peters, 1986b).

A second preliminary point to be made is that there has been relatively little theoretical development concerning the relationship of political executives and career civil servants. This statement is true for individual nations and is especially true of comparative studies of their interactions. There is certainly no shortage of studies of higher civil servants, and there are a large number of studies of political executives, but it is fair to say that much less has been done to analyze patterns of interactions between these two sets of actors in the policymaking process (but see Campbell, 1983; Kaufman, 1981b). There are, of course, some notable exceptions, such as the work of Robert Putnam and his collaborators and Hugh Heclo's work on the United States, but the majority of evidence about the relationships of ministers and their civil servants is anecdotal (Aberbach, Putnam, and Rockman, 1981; Anton, 1980; Eldersveld, Hubee-Boonzaijer, and Kooiman, 1975; Heclo, 1977). Much of this evidence has come from the writings of retired ministers, for example, Richard Crossman, Barbara Castle, Lord Crowther-Hunt, Michael Blumenthal, Califano (Bonafede, 1979; Califano, 1981; Crossman, 1975, 1977; Kellner and Crowther-Hunt, 1980; Young and Sloman, 1982, 1984). This is the principal type of evidence available for some of the points that I will make, and it is itself quite valuable for understanding those points. There is a need, however, to place that evidence within broader analytic and comparative frameworks. This chapter will make a preliminary attempt at such organization and analysis. In it, I will focus to some extent on our knowledge about civil servants and political executives in the United States, but I will then consider comparative frameworks to illuminate the generic pheomenon with which we are concerned.

148

Five Models of Interaction

My statement above that theoretical work concerning the relationships of senior civil servants and political executives has been relatively absent may seem excessively harsh and ill informed. One can discern in the literature, in fact, five very basic models, each extreme in its own way, of the relationship between civil servants and their nominal political masters. These models have only occasionally been consciously articulated as such, and consequently we have been forced to extract and synthesize from the literature in order to present them in a more explicit form. In addition, models have usually been discussed singly rather than as a set. Furthermore, as I have noted, these models are to some degree extreme and in several instances approach ideal-type constructions which illuminate the real world by abstracting from it and providing a standard against which we may compare reality. Few, if any, systems of executive politics in the real world will fit these models exactly. Moreover, almost any national or subnational system will at times display some characteristics of each of the models. I hope, however, that by developing these models and explicitly exploring some apparent relationships with other characteristics of executive politics I can advance our understanding of politics within the executive branch in a number of different countries.

The Formal Model

The first of the models of interaction is the formal-legal model, in which the civil servant in policymaking is reduced to saying "Yes, Minister." This model has been developed in a less formal sense in the United States than in other countries (perhaps especially the United Kingdom), but it has certainly been clearly articulated. The Wilsonian approach to public administration stressed this strictly administrative conception of the role of the civil servant (Wilson, 1887). Interestingly, how-

ever, the separation posited by Wilson served to give civil servants greater room to use their skills without political
contamination (Doig, 1983). Furthermore, numerous statements appearing in the popular media alleging that inappropriate powers were being granted to bureaucrats in making policy
and the related loss of democratic control show that this model
has a place in the popular mind. Indeed, many attempts to reform the executive branch of government have been oriented
toward improving the control of the president and his appointees over permanent civil servants within the executive
branch (Arnold, 1976; Nathan, 1975).

The formal-legal model is obviously a caricature of the role
of bureaucrats and ministers in making policy; it probably was
so even as Wilson and Weber wrote about the respective roles
as they conceived of them (Page, 1985). This model is, however,
important as a normative standard against which to compare
real patterns of interaction and policymaking. Putnam's conception (1973) of the "classical bureaucrat," for example, has
been shown to be a useful standard against which to compare
the attitudes of real-world bureaucrats in a number of countries. And this model also serves as a useful fiction, allowing
civil servants a great deal of functional responsibility while
keeping political responsibility in the hands of elective executive officials (Peters, 1984:31–36). Finally, this model is, despite its caricature in the eyes of the more detached analysts in
academe, one which many real-world executives—especially
political executives—carry with them when they go to work in
government. That they do carry it with them can, of course,
present a great deal of difficulty for those political executives
and may account for much of their reported frustration with
the difficulties in exercising the powers of their office.

The Village Life Model

A second model of the relationship between civil servants
and political executives might be termed the *village life model*.
Although Heclo and Wildavsky (1974) applied the term specifi-

cally to the values of British civil servants working within the Treasury, rather than to the relationship of those civil servants to their political "masters," the idea of an integration of values through socialization and recruitment appears quite applicable to the analysis of political and bureaucratic elites. In this second model, senior civil servants and political executives are conceptualized as having relatively similar values and goals, with the most important perhaps being the maintenance of the government and the smooth functioning of the executive branch (Gournay, 1984; Mayntz, 1984). In this conception of executive branch politics, the political and bureaucratic elites coalesce against outside interference in their own tightly constrained little world. One scholar has gone so far as to advocate the development of a field of "executive-bureaucratic politics" (Szablowski, 1981). He argues that the views and interests of the two sets of actors at the top of organizational pyramids are sufficiently similar to make their interactions, and the pattern of policies which emerges, more readily explicable when they are examined as one group rather than as two. Such a conceptualization would, of course, conform rather closely to the arguments of various elite-theory and Marxist critiques of contemporary capitalist societies as being dominated by a single class which seeks to maintain its own interests rather than following the tenets of democratic theory and the guidelines of mass opinion (Gough, 1979).

A second point of similarity between the two sets of elites is their common interest in the management of the state (Neustadt, 1973). Both sets of executives find it advantageous to advance their careers through effective management and appropriate decisionmaking. Again, however, this point of similarity may vary considerably across political systems and across individuals and structural positions within political systems. This conception of the role of the civil servant is likely to be most pronounced in political systems, for example, continental Europe or Japan, with a well-developed sense of the state. Furthermore, political systems in these places tend to have high levels of interchange between political and administrative careers (see below), so that no artificial barriers have developed. If the advocates of greater politicization of the civil services have their way, there will be pressures for other governments to develop along the same lines into "villages."

Another way of looking at this etatist, or village life model, is as an essentially managerial stance on the part of both politicians and civil servants in the upper reaches of government. An American political executive is more likely to regard management as an important demand of his or her job, everything else being equal, than would a British, Canadian, or European counterpart. This statement might be especially true of the assistant secretaries who are close to the day-to-day management of their organizations and who must demonstrate managerial abilities in order to further their careers (Murphy, Nuechterlein, and Stupak, 1978). Within the upper-echelon bureaucracy in the United States, Heclo (1977:151–52) reported the presence of a number of "institutionalists," whose primary goal appeared to be the effective management of their organization and of government in general. Szablowski (1981) regards these managerial values and interests as rather more broadly distributed throughout the public services. He has argued that, for political executives of the four countries he has studied, almost all of those occupying such positions have very strong managerial and etatist values.

Finally, as I mentioned briefly above, it is important to note that in many political systems the administrative and political career structures are not as isolated and distinct as is sometimes assumed. In fact, the separation which is assumed to exist between those roles is often an extrapolation of the British experience or an extrapolation from normative writing on the politics—administration dichotomy. In the United States, for example, the absence of a higher civil service, in the sense of the term in the European context, has resulted in substantial overlap between administrative and political officials, and at times the functional responsibilities of the two groups may be similar (Heclo, 1984). In France, although the *grand corps* consists of career civil servants, they move freely from administrative to political positions and function as an all-purpose elite for French society, in both the public sector and the private (Suleiman, 1974, 1985). Likewise, a large number of West German politicians are civil servants on leave from the civil service but able to return (Derlien, 1985). Because civil service rank and status in most European countries go with the individual, not with the particular position being held, it is quite possible for these individuals to move freely from politics to administration and back again. Therefore, to some degree, the distinction sometimes drawn between the two career structures may be overly sharp, and the same individuals may simply wear different hats at various stages of their own careers as the leaders of their country.

It is important to keep in mind, however, that, in general, politicians and administrators do have different careers and different occupational perspectives. They are, as Olsen described them, "different players on the same team" (1983:120). The differences are very often in terms of time. The politician has a short time within which to reach his or her goals, while the career bureaucrat may have a lifetime.

The Functional Model

The third model of the relationships between civil servants and politicians we will be considering is, to some extent, an extension of the village life model but with one important difference. While the village life model assumes an integration of political and administrative elites throughout the upper echelons of government, the functional village life model will posit instead an integration among elites along functional lines. There would be close ties among civil servants and political executives within the same functional area (for example, health, education, or defense) and links to other actors in that issue area, such as legislative committees and interest groups. There would be little or no linkage to other civil servants or other political elites outside that issue area. Thus this third model would bear some resemblance to numerous descriptions of corporatism or neocorporatism in a number of European countries and especially to the literature on "iron triangles," "cozy little triangles," or "issue networks" in American politics (Freeman, 1965; Heclo, 1978; Rose, 1980). The model of relationships in which we are interested need not carry along with it all the intellectual baggage associated with those other terms, but a number of points of similarity are interesting and important.

The implications for politics of the functional village life model, or simply the functional model, are rather different from those of the village life model. In the village life model the elite integration described was centered around the values of an upper echelon of public executives (both permanent and political), so that there was an attempt to differentiate "us" from "them" solely on the basis of position within government; it was a horizontally interconnected elite whose principal interest appeared to be the smooth functioning of the political system. This implies a certain absence of content; "whatever is best administered is best governed." Such an arrangement need not be totally devoid of content, but there is a tendency to stress form over substance. One may hear in this at least a faint echo of many of the critiques which have been leveled at the Whitehall system of governance in the United Kingdom (Chapman, 1978; Hoskyns, 1983; Kellner and Crowther-Hunt, 1980; and many others).

The functional model, on the other hand, is oriented toward vertical integration and more extensive contacts with the society as a whole—or at least with specified segments of that society. In such a model of executive interactions, political and administrative elites within a specific policy sector will be allied against political and bureaucratic elites from other policy sectors. The conflicts which are expected to arise would be over money, personnel, legislative time and all the other factors which give one agency or policy precedence over another (Natchez and Bupp, 1973). In these political encounters, policy and organization are more central than elite status or conflict reduction.

The village life and the functional models need not be mutually exclusive, of course, and in the real world are frequently closely intertwined. Although conflicts over policy and money such as those described above may occur within the executive elites, there is a tendency to attempt to contain them and to present a united front to outsiders, especially in political systems with a parliamentary form of government where, despite sharp internal battles (both within a cabinet and between cabinet and civil servants), once a decision has been taken, a relatively united front must be presented to outsiders. It may be hypothesized, in fact, that only the type of elite integration described as the village life model would permit sharp disagreements over policy to be fought out without severe threats to stability, not to mention individual careers. Disagreements may be permitted as long as they are kept in house and are confined to those who are all a part of the small, integrated group which governs.

The Adversarial Model

The fourth model is, to a great extent, the converse of the village life model. It is perhaps the most commonly articulated model of the interactions of these two sets of policymakers. This is the adversarial model, in which the political executive and the senior civil servant are assumed to be competitors for power and control over policy. In this model the civil servant frequently is cast in the position of saying "No, Minister" or, more commonly, of saying nothing at all and proceeding to do whatever he or she thinks best (Young and Sloman, 1982, 1984). This model can be taken seriously even if the reader does not take the politics/administration dichotomy seriously. Even if the two activities are inextricably intertwined, the individuals who occupy positions within either career structure may still regard themselves as competing for power with the incumbents of the other career structure. Most commonly, the model has been articulated as showing the political executive attempting to recapture his or her own organization from the grip of its civil servants. Civil servants might argue, however, that they need to protect their departments from being captured by outsiders who do not understand either the policies

155

being administered or the procedures through which they are administered.

The conflict which is recognized as a part of the adversarial model may arise in one of several ways. One is simply passive or unintended conflict. The bureaucracy, like the mountain, is there and thereby is a challenge to an incoming political executive. Even if the bureaucracy—or more exactly a particular organization—or an individual civil servant does not oppose the policy ideas of the political executive, inertia and the persistence of old habits may make change difficult. Policies may be labeled infeasible simply because things have not been done that way before. Any political executive who comes to office expecting to change policy quickly will rapidly be disappointed (Bonafede, 1979; Rowan, 1979).

The adversarial relationship between the bureaucracy and the political executive may be more active and intentional. This more purposeful conflict may arise from several sources. The most frequent is differences of opinion about the content of specific public policies. As I have noted in other writings, organizations do have ideologies that specify the manner in which policies should be designed and implemented, and the ideas in question may well differ from those of the political executives (Peters, 1981). In such situations, there will typically be conflict over the shape of policy, frequently followed by a period in which the bureaucracy will delay and attempt to outlast the politician. Especially skillful and persistent political executives may be needed to overcome a civil service staff which has decided to dig in and outwait its nominal political masters.

A second source of conflict is the survival of the organization. The one quality which civil servants tend to regard as most crucial in their political masters is the ability to win battles for their organization in the areas of budgets, personnel, and policy issues considered important by members of the organization. Consequently, civil servants will tend not to support a political executive they regard as weak or ineffective in dealing with other politicians and may actively work to have the person removed (Heclo and Wildavsky, 1974:134–38). And perhaps the greatest faux pas which a political executive can perform is to argue for the abolition of the organization, as Terrel Bell did at the U.S. Department of Education (*Washington Post*, 7 August, 1981). This is a sure means of engendering conflict with the civil service staff of the organization.

Finally, there may be real partisan conflict over policy between civil servants and political executives. Given that there are differing career structures, as I have stressed, with that of the civil servant being characterized by political neutrality in many countries, partisan conflict may be a doubtful proposition. But, as I have also pointed out, it is rather easy for civil servants to become politicized. This politicization may be inadvertent, as when a single political party is in office for a long period of time. When there is a change in ruling parties, the civil service is frequently found to be populated largely by individuals who agree with the policies of the previous government. This preponderance need not be the result of an attempt to pack the civil service with opponents of any alternative government. Rather, it may be simply the function of patterns that selectively attract to the civil service individuals who believe in the program of the government in office. Consequently, the bourgeois coalition coming to power in Sweden after more than three decades of Social Democratic government might have had cause to question the willingness of the bureaucracy to cooperate with any policy changes. And the Nixon administration in the United States expressed a belief that the social service departments of government were loaded with Democrats who had been attracted to government during the Kennedy and Johnson administrations (Aberbach and Rockman, 1976). The Reagan administration has made similar arguments about a number of agencies, perhaps most notably the Environmental Protection Agency. The transition may be just as difficult when it is from a conservative to a socialist government, as François Mitterand and his government have discovered in France (Stevens, 1985).

Also, civil servants may accept political tasks. There are provisions in the West German administrative structure for civil servants to take on political tasks, although they accept the possibility of being retired when there is a change in government or even a change in a minister (Derlien, 1985; Mayntz, 1984). And Heclo calls attention to the number of civil servants in the United States who are in political posts, at least on temporary assignments (Heclo, 1977). The provisions of the Civil Service Reform Act of 1978 make political posts even more likely, and these provisions have been used widely by the Reagan administration as a means of increasing their influence over the permanent civil service. The literature abounds with examples of civil servants who were attracted by the glamor of politics, flew too close to the fire, and were eventually burned by their political attachments. Sir William Armstrong's involvement with the Heath government in the United Kingdom is an important case in point (Kellner and Crowther-Hunt, 1980:184–85).

Finally, the civil service may become politicized and partisan because of actions taken by a government concerning the civil service itself. The attacks on civil service pay and perquisites by the Reagan administration and the reactions by the federal civil service represent one example (Peters, 1986b). The more extreme example is the Thatcher government in the United Kingdom. There issues of pay have been combined with conflicts over unionization of workers at the Government Communications Headquarters (GCHQ) to produce very strong civil service reactions against the government. Reactions against the personnel policies may be translated into political opposition to all government policies.

When conflicts based upon partisan allegiances and identifications arise, it might be possible to dismiss these simply as partisan rather than as a part of the patterns of institutional politics we have been discussing. Given the civil service status of at least one set of actors involved, however, it is not so easy to dismiss them except perhaps when civil servants adopt manifestly political stances. The civil servants are still civil servants and can wrap themselves in the legal cloak of civil service protections while also claiming to be above politics. The civil service status and the intermingling of institutional and partisan conflict will make the task of the political executive faced with recalcitrant individuals and organizations all the more difficult.

The Administrative State Model

A fifth model of the interactions between administrative and political executives is termed the administrative state model. This model reflects an increasingly common perception that the decisionmaking of government is dominated by the bureaucracy. I have explored some of the implications of the model rather fully elsewhere and will not belabor the points made there (Peters, 1981). The fundamental conception embodied in the model is that, because of the increasing work load being placed upon governments—even deregulation requires a great deal of effort—and because of the complexity and technical content of that work load, the bureaucracy has come to dominate decisionmaking. This is an important position on institutional politics in contemporary political systems. Legislative bodies or essentially amateur political executives do not have the numbers or capabilities to handle the work load required of modern government, and consequently the important work on policy is left to the permanent civil service (Castles and Wildemann, 1986; Rose, 1974:379–426). Certainly legislatures still pass laws, and their appointees are still nominally in charge of government, but all of the political actors may ultimately be in the control of a bureaucracy with greater access to information upon which to base decisions. The bureaucracy also controls much of the procedural machinery of government and can structure, accelerate, or delay decision through its mastery of procedures. This model does not depend upon a conscious plot by the career civil service, nor is it necessarily a condemnation of bureaucracy. Most of the abdication of authority by political leaders can be seen as voluntary and perhaps even as serving the public interest if technically superior decisions are the result. This model of decisionmaking in modern governments, however, is quite different from that found in most textbooks on democratic government and is almost the exact opposite of the formal-legal model discussed above.

The differences between the adversarial model and the administrative state model may appear rather slight, but they are important. In the adversarial model, it is assumed that political executives are still the prime mover in the decisions which are taken and that the moral imprimatur coming from the electoral process will give these individuals great powers. The bureaucrat is seen as a contender for power based primarily upon technical information, mastery of procedures, and simple longevity in office. In the adversarial model, it is assumed that one side or the other will "win" at different times, depending upon the nature of the conflict and the mobilization on each side's respective resources at that particular time. In the administrative state model, finally, the bureaucracy is visualized as finally victorious, with the political executives and the legislature, as Grosser put it, no more than "participants in a process of registration" (quoted in Dogan, 1975:7). It is important to remember, however, that both of these intellectual constructs model a much more complex reality, so that they will exist primarily in the minds of and the words of detached analysts.

Summary

The five models of interactions among bureaucrats and political executives are, as I have noted, somewhat akin to ideal-type models; no system of government will display all of the patterns of behavior outlined. Page's (1985) very interesting analysis details the extent to which the formal-legal model describes empirical reality. Both national systems and the relationships of individual ministers and civil servants may contain some elements of all the models and may also change rapidly, depending upon the issues or the individuals involved. By using these models, however, we are attempting to illuminate and understand the complexity of the real world.

Characteristics of the Five Models

On the basis of the brief descriptions of each model presented above, as well as other writings concerning these patterns of interaction, we can isolate several dimensions which should further illuminate the differences among these intellectual models. Table 22 presents a simplified description of the five models of interaction in terms of five dimensions. These dimensions should capture the major differences between the five models and could serve as a guide if empirical observations of such systems of interaction were to be performed. I do not, however, presume to present any clear coding rules for categories that are essentially nominal and descriptive.

The first dimension is labeled *tone*, for the want of a better term, to describe something of the general tenor of the interactions among the participants. Four of the five models are described as having a rather smooth or integrated pattern of interaction. As we should have expected, the tone of the adversarial model is much sharper and combative. The tone need not be as combative as the incident recounted in the British Broadcasting Corporation radio series entitled "No, Minister," in which a permanent secretary recalled the occasion when his minister threw the telephone at a shocked civil servant (the permanent secretary commented that his cricket training had helped him field the telephone). The participants in such a system, however, can be expected to display some suspicion and some difficulties in working relationships. Such working relationships are important for humane reasons, but they are also important for the successful management of the organization. Also, more conflictual systems may tend to build in excessive redundancies, checks and counterchecks which will slow down the execution of policies and may even prevent the implementation of a policy in anything approaching the form intended (White, 1969).

The second dimension of variation concerns the identity of the winner in the political process which occurs within the executive branch. Clearly, if the formal/legal model is seen as the most appropriate, the political executives will be masters

Table 22. Characteristics of Ideal-Type Models of Interactions

	Tone	Winners	Conflict resolution	Style	Impacts
Formal/legal	Integrative	Politicians	Command	Authority	Variability
Village life	Integrative	Both	Bargaining	Mutuality	Management
Functional village life	Integrative	Both	Bargaining	Expertise	Interest dominance
Adversarial	Adversarial	???	Power	Conflict	Variability
Administrative state	Integrative	Civil service	Abdication	Expertise	Stability

over policy. In that model the political leaders have the task of shaping decisions, while the bureaucrat must implement those decisions. At the other end of the spectrum, the administrative state model would have the bureaucrats as the real makers and implementers of policy, while politicians would be useful primarily in the legitimation of their actions rather than as really important in making decisions. For two of the models outlined, both political and bureaucratic elites are equal victors in the process but are victors against possible intruders rather than against each other. In both the village life and the functional models, the two elites coalesce at the expense of other elites. In the village life model they coalesce against legislators and other groups in the society in order to maintain their privileged position in government. The functional model allows for a good deal more openness to societal influences than does the village life model, but there is still an attempt to partition one portion of government off from others. Finally, the adversarial model predicts no particular winner in all cases. Instead, winners and losers are determined by the specific set of issues and conditions existing at the time.

The third dimension to be considered in the description of these models of interaction is the style of conflict resolution practiced by the participants in the networks of institutional politics. Again, the formal model is the easiest to describe, with conflicts being resolved almost automatically through law and hierarchical command—"Yes, Minister" in the form accepted of conflict resolution. Again, at the other end of the spectrum, in the administrative state model, conflict is resolved or avoided through the virtual abdication of policy-making responsibilities by elective or appointive political executives in favor of the public bureaucracy. This abdication may not be conscious, but it is nonetheless real. In the village life and functional models, conflict resolution is conducted through bargaining. Given that these two models assume a high degree of integration and common interest in maintaining the elite's interests against real or imagined threats from outsiders, the best means of dealing with conflict is to bargain. Such bargaining might occur within the elite as a whole or within a particular subset of the elite, depending upon the perspective adopted. And the integration of values of the elite members—be it systemwide or functional—will facilitate the bargaining and will also limit the scope of the conflict which emerges to more narrow and technical issues.

The fourth dimension of importance in describing the patterns of interaction between political and bureaucratic executives is the *style* of interaction and thereby essentially the style in which politics is conducted. Within both the functional and the administrative state models, this interaction occurs on the basis of expertise. In both of these systems of interaction, the important attribute is expert knowledge of the policy area. Participants in the functional model use expert knowledge to exclude potential interlopers into their policy area, while those in the administrative state model can use expertise to counteract and formal-legal powers of their political masters. We would expect the formal power, of course, to be manifest in the formal/legal model, in which the legitimate ruling status of the political executive is accepted by the bureaucrat. In the village life model, the acceptance of mutual elite status, the ability to use this status, and the associated personal and professional contacts give the residents of the "village" great power over any potential competitors for power. Finally, power and the ability to muster any weapons available—including such things as formal position and policy expertise, which I have already mentioned—are the medium of exchange in the adversarial model. On any particular issue, either of the sets of actors may be able to muster differing amounts of their own resources in order to be able to "win" that policy conflict.

Finally, there is the dimension of the *impacts* of these differing systems of interaction on the policies adopted by government. For two of the systems, the effects on policy would be hypothesized to be quite variable. If the formal model were to operate as it is alleged to, and if there were alternation in office in a democratic political system, then changes in governing political parties should produce changes in policy. There is, of course, strong evidence to indicate that policy cannot be so readily changed. Likewise, if the adversarial model allows one of the two sets of contending elites to win on different issues at different times, as I indicated above, we should expect variability in policies. This variability would, of course, be compounded by the variability in political party control which would determine the policies stressed by the political executives office, as in the formal model. In contrast, the policies emerging from the administrative state model should be expected to be rather stable. The permanent civil service would be in charge and would tend to preserve much of the status quo despite any attempts of political executives to produce change. Still, bureaucrats are not of course totally devoid of ideas for change and improvement themselves. Some have argued that these ideas arise totally from self-interest (for larger budgets), while others have argued that the ideas arise from professional training and from a sincere interest in improving society (Niskanen, 1971; Rourke, 1979). For whatever reasons they do propose ideas, however, bureaucrats can serve as sources of policy change. Changes proposed by civil servants tend to occur within the context of an existing policy paradigm and typically constitute only incremental departures from the status quo, but they are changes nonetheless. We can expect to find the village life model associated with policy stability also, although much of the concern of the participants in such an arrangement would be for systematic management that does not rock the boat rather than on altering the details of operating policies (Heclo and Wildavsky, 1974). And finally, although the policies adopted through a functional model may be quite similar to those which would be found in the administrative state model, there should be greater impact of the connections to groups in the society than would be the case with the administrative state model.

Explaining Types of Executive Systems

I should again emphasize that in the real world it may be difficult to distinguish these patterns of interaction from one another neatly and clearly, especially without empirical research directly related to the topic. These dimensions should provide some ideas, however, regarding the types of factors which we must consider when we attempt to distinguish among the several models, and they can be considered hypotheses about the effects of a particular pattern of elite interaction on the policies adopted by government. Yet another question remains, however: what factors might predict the development of one pattern versus another in different political systems or within components of a single government? Obviously, there are a huge number of such factors—some of which will be personal and idiosyncratic—and to isolate the effects of any single factor in such a diffuse and complex pattern of interaction is a difficult logical problem. We can generate a set of hypotheses and muster some corroborating evidence, however, that may assist in clarifying this one crucial arena of policymaking as it fits within the overall pattern of policymaking and administrative behavior in Western industrialized societies.

Issues

Perhaps the presence of one pattern of interaction or another could be explained by specific issues being considered. This type of explanation might be useful for only a limited range of issues. The clearest type of issue affecting patterns of interaction between civil servants and political executives would be one which clearly affects the civil service as an institution, for example, pay, perquisites, or unionization. In these cases one should expect either the adversarial model or the administrative state model to develop. Which one did develop would depend, of course, upon the strength of the political executives and a number of other factors that I will discuss in this catalog of hypotheses, but the important point here is that an issue of this type will clearly pit the bureaucracy and those who might wish to control it against one another. Also, as some issues of this type can become highly politicized, for example, unionization and pay comparability with the private sector, the boundaries of the conflict may be extended to the broader social and political arena, generally giving political executives additional resources in their struggles to control the bureaucracy (Peters, 1984:189–96). Attempts by public employees to use their organizational power tend to provoke public resentment and to provide support for political executives.

Another aspect of an issue which may be hypothesized to be related to the pattern of interaction between civil servants and political executives would be the technical content of that interaction. The more technical the issue, the more power the permanent bureaucracy would tend to have, and consequently the more the interaction pattern would tend to approximate that of the administrative state model. As noted above, bureaucratic control of information will have the determining influence on many decisions in government (Jackson, 1982; Niskanen, 1971; Tullock, 1965). Political executives may attempt to counterattack through the use of personal advisers, appointive committees, and the like, but the civil service will still tend to be dominant. We should note that many decisions over which the bureaucracy has a controlling influence will provide little direct benefit to the civil servants, and they may gain nothing except the good feeling that a job has been well done (Hood, Huby, and Dunsire, 1984). They will control decisions nonetheless, however, and a feeling of technical mastery may be all that they sought from the outset.

Finally, the degree of public concern, and especially organized public concern, over a particular issue will influence patterns of interaction. If the issue is considered important by an organized group in the society, and there are means of group access to government, then something approaching the functional model of interactions is likely to develop, especially if a stable pattern of interaction among concerned groups—civil servants, political executives, legislative actors, and the interest groups—has developed which would facilitate early consultation and a policy proposal acceptable to all concerned. In the dynamics of the functional model, the political executive would be most likely to be the outsider, especially if there has been a recent change in the party controlling government. It is

quite possible in such a case that the functional model of interaction would evolve into the adversarial, with the civil service
and its pressure group allies confronting the novice political
executive. This outcome would be especially likely if the party
coming into power had made campaign commitments to alter
the practice in the policy area in question or if it had ideological predispositions which would be hostile to the interest
groups in the area. The experience of the Reagan administration in the United States, the Thatcher government in the
United Kingdom, and the Mitterand government in France all
supply useful evidence on this topic (Peters, 1986b; Stevens,
1985).

The Political Executives

Another factor which would be hypothesized to affect the
pattern of interaction between civil servants and the political
world in which they live is the nature of both the political executives and the bureaucrats. Both sets of actors in these inter-
changes have characteristics which will affect their interaction
with the other, and arguably political executives will vary less
than the bureaucratic executives and the bureaucratic systems
with which they interact. The patterns of recruitment of political executives and their involvement in the policy process appear to vary less than the bureaucratic systems, which vary
rather greatly, but important differences in the nature of political executives will still influence their effectiveness and their
mode of interaction with civil servants.

One such factor is simply the number of political executives.
The numbers of American and British political appointees have
been compared several times (Neustadt, 1973). When a change
of governing party occurs in the United Kingdom, only several
hundred people lose jobs, whereas in the United States several
thousand lose jobs. With more political executives active in
government, there would naturally be a greater attempt on the
part of the executives to control the direction of government
policy; otherwise, why are executives there? Still, we should

count not only the number of readily identifiable political executives occupying formal governmental positions. Frequently an apparently small number of political leaders will surround themselves with a number of advisers and associates who may not occupy any formal position, who may be paid out of either public or private funds and who may increase substantially the capability of the political executive to exercise control or at least to compete for control. Thus, ministers who have the assistance of bodies such as *cabinets* and personal secretaries would be more likely to engage in adversarial relationships with the permanent civil service than would the average minister in British government, who has little personal assistance other than that provided by civil servants (Klein and Lewis, 1977). Even British government, however, is now more populated with advisers than it was in earlier years, and Mrs. Thatcher in particular seeks advice from outside the civil service (Hoskyns, 1983; Jones, 1985).

A second characteristic of political executives influencing their patterns of interaction with the civil service is the type of training they have received and their career patterns. Here we can easily contrast the generalist orientation of British political executives with the more specialized selection of executives in the United States, West Germany, or Sweden (Lundquist and Stahlberg, 1983; Mayntz, 1980). Generalists will be less able to contest issues on substantive grounds than political executives with more specialized training or at a minimum a career pattern which forces them to specialize early in their careers. Generalist political executives may thus be expected to be associated with the administrative state or village life models of interaction, depending upon several other factors. They may also be found associated with the functional patterns of interaction although very much as junior partners of the more specialized civil servants and interest group leaders in these subsystems.

A third characteristic of political executives which may be hypothesized to affect their interactions with civil servants is the fundamental form of government in their country. The demands of cabinet government and collective responsibility may require the political elites to take a more adversarial stance vis-à-vis civil servants than would be true in other forms of government. Furthermore, cabinet government may, because of the apparently closer connection between electoral choice and those occupying office, entail pressures toward the formal/legal pattern of interaction, especially when the minister is considered to have very pervasive responsibilities for the activities of the department, whether or not the extreme position is actually carried out in practice (Wright, 1980).

Another factor affecting executive interactions, not unrelated to the impact of parliamentary government, is the role conception of political executives. Principally, this is a question of whether they regard themselves first as politicians or first as policymakers and departmental managers. It may be difficult to unravel these two strands in the role of the political executive, although several interesting studies have been made on this subject. Headey, for example, has discussed a variety of roles which ministers in Britain's government have adopted for themselves, and Putnam and his associates have provided some information concerning the attitudes and role perceptions of politicians who are in frequent contact with civil servants (Anton, 1980:85–94; Headey, 1974). I would hypothesize that an executive who construed his or her role as that of the politician might adopt relatively simplistic conceptions of the relationship with bureaucrats, either adopting a formal/legal conception of their relationships or gratefully accepting the administrative state model and leaving all the nasty work of running the ministry to the permanent staff.

Political executives who regarded their tasks as policy entrepreneurs or as managers would be more likely to engage in some form of conflict with the civil service; if their external job experiences made them members of larger issue networks, they might well adopt a functional village life conception of the role of political executives. Such role distinctions have a great deal to do with career patterns in political and social life, just as did the earlier distinction between generalist and specialist patterns of training in the relationship between ministers and civil servants. If the criterion for recruitment of political executives is the ability to pacify one wing of the party or another, or the ability to win a certain type of constituency, the behavior of the executives in office will be very different from that of people selected for their knowledge of a particular type of policy. Clearly those who regard themselves as policy entrepreneurs will be more interested in engaging in conflicts over policy than would those who think of their role primarily as political and electoral. Policy and electoral success may of course be closely related, but individual political elites may stress one rather than the other, and the emphasis can affect their interactions with their bureaucratic staff members.

Finally, the openness of the government and its ministries to the organized groups in society will influence the manner of interaction of political elites and their civil servants. This is, of course, in some ways almost a definition of the functional model outlined previously, but the influences may extend beyond this one model. If there is a general openness to interest group influence, and if political executives tend to be recruited from different career structures and lack a close connection with societal interests, then one might expect an adversarial relationship rather than a functional pattern of interaction. On the other hand, if the political system is not generally open and accepting of interest group influences, the possibility for developing the elitist village life pattern of interactions is that much greater.

The training, careers, and role conceptions which political executives bring with them to office will, as we have shown, tend to influence the manner in which they interact with the permanent civil service staff that they find when they come to office. More important, this background may influence the effectiveness of executives in performing the tasks that they were elected or appointed to perform. The adversarial model is, as noted previously, perhaps the most commonly articulated model of interaction, but it is not necessarily the most effective. On the other hand, the political executive who comes to office ignorant of the responsibilities that he or she must perform and of issues in the policy area is not likely to further the cause of democracy. Still, the effectiveness of the political executives in implementing policies will to some degree depend upon the characteristics of the civil servants with whom they must interact.

The Civil Service

At this point we should consider some of the characteristics of civil servants and bureaucratic systems which influence their interactions with their political "masters." Perhaps because of our own training and interests, there does appear to be more variability in bureaucratic systems than among political executives. The differences can, however, be subsumed into several subcategories of characteristics.

Training. One of the principal factors affecting the relationships among civil servants and their political executives is the type of training received by civil servants. Different countries have developed a variety of patterns in the training of their civil servants which may be hypothesized to affect relationships with political executives. One such pattern might be termed the Oxbridge pattern, after the two major British universities which have traditionally provided (and continue to provide) a disproportionate share of higher civil servants—as well as political executives—for the British government. The training which these future executives receive has generally little to do with the roles they will occupy later in their careers but has been oriented toward the humanities (Garrett, 1980). This pattern of training has tended to create a tightly integrated elite with relatively little substantive training in any particular policy area. It also makes the upper civil service and political executives more similar than different. In short, such a pattern of training should be conducive to the development of the village life model detailed earlier: that model is, to some degree, itself abstracted from British government.

A second pattern, which is characteristic of much of continental Europe, is the use of law as a background for the civil service. The modal German, Austrian, Dutch, or Scandinavian civil servant will have taken a degree in law before entering the upper civil service. This legalism in training tends to carry over into job performance, so that there is perhaps a greater tendency toward adopting the formal/legal model in such systems than there would be otherwise (Steinkemper, 1974). The legal statement of the relationship between civil servants and politicians in almost all political systems is that political leaders are to make policy decisions and the civil service is to implement them. Training in the legal tradition may make the civil servant more willing to accept this formalistic conception of the role. It certainly should not be inferred that West German or Scandinavian civil servants are robots blindly following the dictates of politicians, and indeed there are numerous examples of conflicts over policy between the two groups, but it does mean that it is easier for a civil servant trained in a legal tradition to accept a more narrowly circumscribed conception of the proper functions of the civil service.

A third pattern of training for civil servants is typified by the École Nationale d'Administration (ENA) in France, in which prospective civil servants receive distinctive schooling above and beyond that received in any postsecondary educational institutions. This training tends to make the upper civil service a class apart, separating the "ENAcrats" both from political executives and from other members of the civil service (Mosher, 1978). Everything else being equal, we would hypothesize, such a pattern of training would tend to differentiate between the higher civil service and political executives and would thus create the conditions for an adversarial relationship between the two groups. We should be quick to note, however, that in the French case the graduates of ENA constitute an elite for the entire social system and tend to infiltrate not only the political executive but the private sector as well (Alphandery et al., 1968:193ff.; Suleiman, 1978:226–35).

Finally, there is a functional pattern of training for the higher civil service. Such training is rarely intentional but is more simply the education in specialties given to students who then later elect to join the civil service. This pattern of training is perhaps best typified by the civil service in the United States, which tends to hire for positions on the basis of some functional expertise (Mosher, 1978). And this tendency will, in turn, produce a civil service which tends to be very well versed in the policies it administers and may well be able to defeat any political elites coming to office that are less well acquainted with those issues. And given that the agencies for which these civil servants will work also tend to have close connections with the interest groups in the respective policy area, they may frequently be part of functional patterns of interaction, with the political executives being perhaps the least important constituents. This pattern has been altering in the direction of a more adversarial model as the development of "issue networks" has produced more knowledgeable political executives (Heclo, 1978; Jordan, 1981).

Careers. The career patterns of civil servants are related to the patterns of training described above and may also independently influence the patterns of interaction between civil servants and political executives. Civil service career patterns routinely differentiate between generalists and specialists. The career patterns fostered by individual administrative systems may either reinforce or counteract the pattern of training received by the civil servant before entry. The training received by British civil servants is quite general, for example, and the career pattern according to which younger civil servants move relatively frequently between jobs reinforces the generalist perspective. On the other hand, although law is an all-purpose, general training for the civil service, once selected, Swedish or Danish civil servants will typically remain within a single organization for a good part or all of their careers.

I would hypothesize that, just as with generalist patterns of training, generalist career patterns tend to create something of a village life relationship between civil servants and political executives. This career pattern reinforces a variety of contacts among the civil service and with political executives and at the same time reduces the commitment of a civil servant to any particular policy area. The generalist career pattern tends to give the individual civil servant some sense of the generic problems of government and may consequently limit his or her willingness to press the claims of one department or agency against the overall demands of centralized control and management (Kellner and Crowther-Hunt, 1980:22–45).

Rather obviously, the specialist career would be hypothesized to produce a rather different pattern of behavior. This pattern might be best exemplified by the civil service system in the Scandinavian countries which, apart from centralized standards for recruiting civil servants, leave the majority of personnel decisions to individual ministries and boards. Although individuals may at some time in their career apply for other positions and receive them, the modal civil servant will spend a career within the single organization. These career patterns, or the somewhat more centralized pattern of recruitment in the United States, might be hypothesized to be related either to an adversarial relationship with political executives or to the functional model of interaction. In either instance, there would not be the integration across agencies that is predicted by a generalist career pattern.

Specialized Bureaucratic Organizations. Several specialized career structures within public bureaucracies may also influence patterns of interaction. Most notably, the corps structures which exist in France, Italy, and Spain may produce highly integrated subsets of individuals within the bureaucracy with a pronounced organizational identity of their own. Particularly in France these civil servants are not confined to their nominal functional designations (for example, the Inspection des Finances is involved with more than just financial probity) but constitute an all-purpose elite for government and the society. The personal contacts, prestige, and knowledge which members of these *grand corps* obtain enables them to manage their own village very well and the entire society not too badly (Suleiman, 1985).

Another specialized structure, although not nearly as clearly defined as the grand corps, is the "superbureaucrats" (Campbell and Szablowski, 1979). These civil servants work for such coordinating organizations within government as the Office of Management and Budget in the United States; the Treasury in the United Kingdom; the Privy Council Office, Treasury Board Secretariat, and so forth in Canada; and the host of other organizations which attempt to coordinate fiscal, personnel, and legal actions across the wide variety of organizations in government. Although a number of career civil servants are employed by these organizations, they stand in a special relationship to politics and are changed with implementing the wishes of a government to perhaps a greater extent than civil servants in operating departments. If the civil servant is willing to accept a position in one of these organizations, he or she is implicitly willing to accept the wishes of their political executives. Furthermore, these civil servants do not have the organizational turf and clientele interest to protect that civil servants in line agencies have; one major part of their functions is to subsume those interests into a broader national interest (as defined by the party in power). Rather obviously, then, civil servants in these central organizations might be expected to engage in the village life relationship with their political masters and to take the part of their central, staff organizations against the interest of line agencies. The idea of village life was developed for the Treasury and may still be especially applicable there and in other elite organizations.

The same reasoning that I have applied to the macro level of government organization might also apply to lower levels of organization. The staff civil servants generally found in most public organizations might be expected to be more likely to accept the viewpoints of the political appointees with whom they work than would members of the line components of these same organizations. Furthermore, as they become identified with the personal viewpoints of one or more political executives, these staff civil servants will quite possibly also have rather briefer careers in their particular positions than would the line civil servants.

Role Conceptions. Finally, as with the political executives, the roles adopted by civil servants in their relationships with political executives manifest an important psychological element. To some extent, these role conceptions will be developed and reinforced by some of the structural factors already mentioned, but they are also the products of cultural patterns in the society (Nachmias and Rosenbloom, 1978). Societies and their members regard hierarchical relationships such as would be found in the formal/legal model quite differently. They also regard conflict among individuals very differently and further develop different mechanisms for coping with potential conflict. Consequently, the interpersonal relationships within organizations will be influenced by such cultural patterns, perhaps especially by the willingness of civil servants to accept the hierarchical authority of someone nominally superior in an organizational chart. There are also differing concepts of just what government and the public sector *mean* that will also have important consequences for the manner in which the government can be managed. In short, the relationships between civil servants and the political master may be a function of what each side believes it should be doing in government.

Conclusion

It is now perhaps obvious to even the casual reader that this book presents more of a research agenda than a formal statement of findings. Its statement of that research agenda, however, is more formalized than the statements of those who study these questions usually are. The understanding of the relationship between members of the executive branch who just happen to have arrived in their position through different routes is quite important for the management of contemporary political systems and for the functioning of political democracy. If electoral politics and the politics within bodies of elective officials in selecting a government are to mean anything, then those who emerge from the selection process must be able to govern. In the majority of cases, however, those who come to office deplore their difficulties in governing. On the other hand, however, an argument can be made in favor of experience and longevity in office and for the continuation of policies which have shown themselves to be at least marginally effective. This conflict between popular choice and stability and between democracy and technocracy motivated some of my concerns in this chapter.

I answered the empirical question raised at the beginning of this chapter at least in part by outlining several models of relationships and by making a number of hypotheses about those models, but the normative and prescriptive problem remains. How can we devise an arrangement which preserves both the values of popular control through the electoral process and the permanence, expertise, and nonpartisan nature of the civil service? The first possible answer is that this agenda is impossible and that those who design the institutions of government should forget about it. A second and only marginally more satisfying answer is that the solution is simply a trade-off. We should perhaps be content with certain institutions, such as the central institutions described above, which are dominated by the will of the elected executives, while expert and permanent civil servants may dominate the majority of line institutions, relatively speaking. The distinction between expert civil servants and amateur but earnest political executives may be excessively simplistic, as many political executives may come to office with substantial knowledge or interest in what they are administering, but the executives may still find themselves considered outsiders simply because they are not members of the organizations on a permanent basis. In general, however, there may be a trade-off between the two sets of values which will provide some guidance in designing institutions and allocating responsibilities among them.

A third proposal which has been made to try to redress any imbalances in power between political and bureaucratic executives is to improve the quality of the executives being recruited. This plea has been made several times in the United States and has also been made in other countries (Lynn, 1981; Malek, 1978; Rose, 1974). The problem is always to obtain political executives who are capable of managing large organizations, have political skills, and have some substantive knowledge about a policy area. If such talented people can be found, they are generally so well paid in the private sector that they cannot be attracted to the public sector. The career structures of government would need to be sufficiently open to allow them to participate, as is now true in the United States but

178

not in countries with more closed personnel systems for the executive branch of government.

On the other hand, the plea has been made to tame the civil service and to place people in charge of organizations who will be subservient to political authority. Here we have almost the reverse of the problem with the political executives. The individuals who rise to the top of the bureaucratic ladder are apparently too talented. This situation is to some extent as it should be, and we as citizens should not want agencies managed by less than completely competent individuals or by individuals who do not have policy ideas and some determination to have those ideas implemented. This statement suggests that a rather basic trade-off is implicit in the role of the public bureaucracy. On the one hand we want it to be docile and subservient to political authority, but on the other hand it should be dynamic, creative, and highly skilled.

The roles being communicated to the members of the executives of industrialized democracies may therefore be contradictory and confusing. We want our political executives to have the best available leadership and managerial talent, but we want to pay them only a pittance compared with their worth in the market and we want to make them responsible to a number of other political forces. Then, too, we want dynamic and aggressive civil servants who will cower when a politician speaks. Until these contradictions can be resolved, the problems of executive leadership in government may well persist.

My original aim of identifying the locus of power in public decisionmaking has been advanced, but perhaps no definitive answers have been given. We do now have a better idea of the possible power relationships among powerful actors in the policymaking process as well as some notions about the factors which may give one side or the other greater power (if indeed there are really identifiable sides).

It remains, however, to undertake a detailed application and testing of these conceptualizations in a truly comparative manner. Thus, unlike the other substantive chapters in this book, chapter 5 has supplied no real data and has not operationalized the research questions posed. As I noted at the beginning of the chapter, however, one means of advancement in areas where empirical research is extremely difficult is just this process of creating more formalized statements about the problem and then marshaling whatever anecdotal and secondary evidence is available. As with the formal economic models discussed in the preceding chapter, this procedure may then provide the theoretical background against which to attempt to marshal "harder" empirical data.

6

Conclusion

This book began with a set of rather simple premises and one even simpler question. The two premises were, first, that the study of public administration was in principle no different from the study of other aspects of political behavior and that, like the other components of governing, it could be better studied from a comparative perspective than from a narrow, national one. The second premise was that there is substantial variation in public administration and public organizations and that they can be studied empirically and quantitatively—again, like any other aspect of political behavior. The measurements which could be used for public administration may not be as obvious and may not have the face validity associated with measures such as votes cast or public expenditures, but they are valid measures nonetheless. Furthermore, where such measures do not exist they must be fostered by scholars concerned with this research topic.

The deceptively simple question which emerged from our deliberations was why comparative public administration has not made the progress in theory development and intellectual respectability within the social sciences that other, similar components of the discipline—most notably comparative public policy studies—have made. Comparative administration showed great promise during the 1960s and 1970s. That promise appears to have been unfulfilled, and little progress has been made in developing the conceptual and theoretical understanding necessary for any further advance. In fairness, a number of important books and monographs have appeared, but little cumulative theoretical development appears to have occurred. While this statement may seem an exaggeration to many observers, it can be argued that the vast majority of the work in this field rather dully describes relatively minor elements of an administrative system in some country or makes predictable normative arguments about the virtues of development administration by those who stand to profit from more funding for it. The real intellectual fire appears to have gone out of the field. Why?

To some degree the answer to the simple question with which we began is the failure to recognize the validity of the premises. With some notable exceptions, many of the scholars involved in comparative public administration appear to have been little interested in the development of the theoretical foundations or of the empirical basis for progress as defined by the contemporary social sciences. This lack of interest was in part a function of much of the training in public administration, which has stressed practice rather than theory and a proper place in academia. In fact, much of the field of public administration has positively deplored the role of theory and has enshrined the role of practice. This emphasis may have been beneficial for students finding a job in the short run, but it has done nothing to improve fundamental understanding of the subject matter at hand. Furthermore, in the long run, such a failure to recharge intellectual batteries in this field of inquiry may undermine its utility for practitioners.

Also, to the extent that students of public administration have been interested in theory, it has been theory (for example, Weber) which stressed the similarity of all public bureaucracies and the empirical and normative inability of all public administrators to behave in an autonomous fashion. Not only were public administration students told that good bureaucrats *should* not make decisions on their own, but they by inference learned that they *could* not make decisions on their own. The conflation of empirical and normative statements left something of a theoretical mortmain on those trained in this field, so that they frequently assumed that very little variation did occur in public bureaucracies. Oddly enough, there *was* very little variation despite the painstaking efforts to describe minute differences in structures and processes. These are important variables for understanding decisionmaking in organizations, but little was done to extend the inquiry to the analysis of decisionmaking.

Finally, and perhaps the greatest indictment, is that there appear to have been inadequate efforts to apply the tools of the contemporary social sciences to the study of public administration. As with most official aspects of the public sector, a big paper trail has been left by those involved in public administration, but it has not been adequately exploited. Certainly, much of these data do not come neatly packaged, and some substantial effort, creativity, and heroic assumptions may be necessary to interpret them, but important comparative research is possible. Public bureaucracies make a huge number of decisions when they make secondary legislation, decide individual eligibility for a variety of government programs, or decide cases in quasi-judicial proceedings. These records need to be exploited to a much greater extent than they have been in the past.

It is now the time, as they say at the poker table, to put up or shut up. What have I contributed to the type of inquiry into comparative public administration that I have been advocating? The four substantive chapters of this book have undertaken both to analyze the possibilities of conducting empirical research on public administration cross-culturally, and to do some empirical research. Inevitably, my review of work done in the past and of the prospect for additional research has been selective and has ignored some publications by colleagues laboring in the vineyard of comparative administration. Nonetheless, the rather gloomy characterization of the field which introduced the book can apparently be defended when the record is examined more closely. There has simply not been the type of theoretically driven and directly comparative research produced that would have advanced the study of administration. With any luck, the research reported here has made some progress toward such advances.

The first research question which I addressed is the seemingly simple question of identifying and describing a public employee in the context of the total labor force. I found that the increasing complexity of the economic and social systems of industrial societies makes it difficult to determine who is employed in the public sector and who is not. In addition, if we begin to look at the number of "industries" in which the public sector is involved, we find an interesting and important mixture of public and private employment even in industries which we tend to regard as peculiarly public. This statement appears to be especially true of the United States but also applies to other industrialized societies. Unless we understand just what the limits of the public sector are, we will make faulty inferences about both the size of the government and the manner in which many goods and services are produced. We consider public safety a governmental function, for example, but there are as many private police officers as public police officers in the United States or more. The research reported in chapter 2 delineated the relationships between the public and the private sectors and examined data on employment in several industrialized societies in addition to the United States. In addition, it has a great deal of relevance for contemporary political debates about the proper role of the public and the private sectors in producing a whole range of public services.

Chapter 3 examined another possible means of defining the public sector, namely by counting the number of public organizations which exist within the context of the total public sector. Again, it is not at all easy to determine just when an organization is within the public sector and when it is not. An increasing number of organizations exist with some of the characteristics of public sector organizations and some characteristics of private sector organizations. In fact, an increasing number of organizations cannot be clearly labeled either public or private. Again, this type of information has considerable importance for contemporary political debates about the size of government and by inference about its proper size.

Not only do we have a question about the identification of organizations in the public sector, but we have a very definite question about the dynamics of growth of the population of organizations in the public sector. It has by now become conventional to think of public organizations as quite permanent and resistant to change. The prevailing idea, however, is based to some degree upon ideological conceptions of the inefficiency and uncontrollability of the public sector and to some degree upon flawed research. Chapter 3 examined the dynamics of change of the population of organizations in the U.S. federal bureaucracy. Its basic finding was that change rather than permanence is the most typical feature of this population of organizations, especially if we consider the full variety of possible changes in a population of organizations and not just dramatic termination events. Furthermore, this finding is more true if we look at the full range of federal organizations rather than at only the major organization such as cabinet departments. In line with these results, we need to develop means of thinking about government and the public bureaucracy which emphasize change and dynamism rather than stability.

The fourth chapter of this book has attempted to understand better the behavior of people who hold positions in the public bureaucracy. A number of questions may be asked about bureaucratic behavior, but there has been relatively little directly comparative research. Some major examples, such as the work of Aberbach, Putnam, and Rockman (1981) and their associates, would seem to belie this generality, as would the research of scholars such as Heclo and Wildavsky (1974), Suleiman (1974, 1978), Olsen (1983), and Campbell and Szablowski (1979). Despite this corpus of research, serious deficiencies still remain in our comparative understanding of the behavior of officials in the public bureaucracy, especially at the very top of the bureaucratic structures, where officials' work is so hidden from the public eye and so enmeshed in institutional understanding that it is difficult for outsiders to comprehend the officials' behavior fully.

One means of approaching the difficult problem of behavior in the public bureaucracy has been to develop highly idealized models of behavior of the participants, especially those at the tops of the hierarchies. A number of such models have been developed, almost all depending upon the formal logic of economics and the assumption of utility maximization in efforts to explain the actions of those in government. The assumption at the heart of these models has been that individuals running government organizations would attempt to maximize the size of their budgets as a means of maximizing their own personal utility. Furthermore, given the opportunity, they would maximize the employment of personnel in the organization as a means either of enhancing their own utility or of increasing the number of voters with a vested interest in the preservation of the bureaucratic institutions.

As interesting and powerful as these models appear to be, they have one serious deficiency: they do not work. Very little of the behavior of public officials appears to be comprehensible within the narrow confines of these models. The motivations of those in bureaucratic office, and the motivations of their "sponsors" in the legislature, are all much more complex than those posited by the formal models. Simplification is an important tool for understanding complex situations, but oversimplification distorts more than it can ever clarify. If the formal models of public bureaucracy do nothing else, however, they permit us to eliminate one characterization of the behavior of public officials and to proceed onward in the attempt to develop more subtle and complex understandings. It is especially important to note that these models do not work very well in the United States, with its highly decentralized public bureaucracy and pervasive belief that people in government do behave in an entrepreneurial fashion to maximize their own benefits from the public budget. Even if they are trying to do so, the evidence we have gathered here is that they are terribly unsuccessful.

Chapter 5 addressed the question of power in government: who rules? In democratic political systems we like to believe that the rulers are those who have been elected in a formal election by the people and those appointed by those who are elected. That is what democratic government is presumed to be all about. In almost all contemporary democracies, however, the question arises as to whether those elected officials or their career civil servants actually exercise the real power over public policy. It is therefore important to attempt to understand the possible roles that civil servants and elected officials can play in modern democracies and what may explain the relative powers of the two sets of policymaking actors.

Chapter 5 developed five alternative models of the relationship between civil servants and their nominal political masters. These range from the formal Weberian and Wilsonian conceptions of the civil servant as a robot following the directives of politicians to a more cynical conception of the bureaucracy actually in charge, with elected officials merely providing a rubber stamp for the public policies adopted. Each of these five models abstracts from reality, just as Weber's basic model of bureaucracy was an abstraction against which to compare the real world. Given the difficulties encountered in measuring or even understanding political power, this may be as good a way as any in the short run to approach the complex problems of modern government. Furthermore, it is especially important as a means of attempting to understand the factors which may account for the differential powers of either politicians or career civil servants in different political systems. This chapter, then, serves as a means of trying to understand the complex world of policymaking and of attempting to sort out who is actually in charge of policy in modern governments. The models developed in this chapter are more political than those discussed in the previous chapter; I hoped that they would make up for in reality what they might lose in precision and in assumed predictive capabilities.

This book may be extremely unsatisfying to many readers. It has, to some degree on purpose, raised more questions than it has been capable of answering. Its premise was the simple observation that the study of comparative public administration has not made the scholarly progress which was promised for it only a few years ago and that it should have done so. The word "should" in this instance has two meanings. The first is that, given the momentum which characterized this field of inquiry only a decade ago, it is quite surprising that more progress has not been made. There has been a great loss of momentum and apparently of intellectual interest in the types of questions we have been raising here.

Should in this context also means that there is a great need to address these questions more thoroughly and competently. Administration is a crucial component of the policymaking process, and the public bureaucracy is a significant political institution. A focus on the "inputs" made to government or on what emerges at the other end of the process in the form of policies cannot really tell us what went on in the process. In particular, neither focus can explain, or help us to grasp, the extremely subtle politics involved in administration and implementation. Without such an understanding, it may not be possible to say that the policy itself is really understood. If we are to have a good comprehension of what actually does occur in government, then we must know what happens as public laws are administered and must comprehend the role of the public bureaucracy in making that law in the first place.

This book makes a beginning effort toward achieving that understanding. Most particularly, we are arguing that we will have no really useful insight without the process of comparison. We may think we understand government and policymaking in our own country, or in some other country which is the major geographical focus of our inquiry, but until we submit that understanding to comparison, we cannot say that we really understand why things work as they do. We may not even after we have made appropriate comparisons, but we would hope to have progressed. If nothing else, the process of comparison forces the scholar to identify what he or she considers to be the most relevant features of the subject of their inquiry.

In addition to emphasizing the need for comparison, I hope that this book has emphasized the need for *systematic* comparison. I have argued that comparative public administration appears to have fallen behind relative to comparative public policy studies in large part because students of policy had ready-made, interval-level measures (public expenditure) that most people working the field could regard as meaningful indicators of the policies and priorities of governments. As a result these researchers were able to begin almost immediately to produce research which conformed to all the principles of good social scientific inquiry. Students of comparative public administration, on the other hand, lacked such measures and must therefore now attempt to develop them.

To that end, each of the four substantive chapters in this book has sought to develop and use quantitative information, or systematic reasoning, to address problems in comparative public administration. In some areas, for example, the enumeration of the population of organizations, this task was easier than in others. In addition, data constraints and the knowledge of the author meant that the book concentrated on data available from the United States and a limited number of European countries. In principle, at least, much of the same type of work could be undertaken in virtually all industrialized and many industrializing countries. Again, the fundamental point is that one way to approach the problem of energizing the study of comparative administration is to make it much more like other components of political science and the social sciences more broadly. This may not be the only avenue to follow in reaching that goal, but it seems to hold a great deal of promise. I hope that the contents of this book have advanced us at least a few yards down that long and difficult road.

References

Aberbach, J. D., R. D. Putnam, and B. A. Rockman (1981). *Bureaucrats and Politicians in Western Democracies.* Cambridge, Mass.: Harvard University Press.

Aberbach, J. D., and B. A. Rockman (1976). Clashing Beliefs within the Executive Branch: The Nixon Administration Bureaucracy. *American Political Science Review* 70:456–68.

Advisory Commission on Federal Pay (1985). *Report on the Fiscal 1985 Pay Increase.* Washington, D.C.: Advisory Committee on Federal Pay.

Ahlbrandt, R. (1973). Efficiency in the Provision of Fire Services. *Public Choice* 16:1–16.

Aldrich, H. E. (1979). *Organizations and Environments.* Englewood Cliffs, N.J.: Prentice-Hall.

Aldrich, H., and E. R. Auster (1986). Even Dwarfs Started Small: Liabilities of Age and Size and Their Strategic Implications. In B. Staw and L. L. Cummings, eds., *Research in Organizational Behavior,* vol. 8. Greenwich, Conn.: JAI Press.

Aldrich, H., and U. H. Staber (1986). How American Business Organized Itself in the Twentieth Century. Paper presented at the annual meeting of the American Sociological Association, New York, August.

Allison, G. T. (1971). *The Essence of Decision.* Boston: Little, Brown.

Almond, G. A., and S. Verba (1963). *The Civic Culture.* Boston: Little, Brown.

Alphandery, C., Y. Bernard, F. Bloch-Lainé, and O. Chevrillon (1968). *Pour nationaliser l'état.* Paris: Editions du Seuil.

Anton, T. J. (1980). *Administered Politics: Elite Political Culture in Sweden.* Boston: Martinus Nijhoff.

Argyris, C. (1964). *Integrating the Individual and the Organization.* New York: Wiley.

Armstrong, J. A. (1973). *The European Administrative Elite.* Princeton: Princeton University Press.

190

References

Arnold, P. E. (1976). The First Hoover Commission and the Managerial Presidency. *Journal of Politics* 38:33–50.

Ashford, D. E. (1981). *Policy and Politics in Britain.* Philadelphia: Temple University Press.

Bargas, D. (1983). Reflexions sur quelques problèmes majeurs du système de rémunération des fonctionnaires de l'état. *Revue française d'administration publique* 28:33–42.

Barker, A. (1982). *Quangos in Britain.* London: Macmillan.

Barnett, J. (1982). *Inside the Treasury.* London: André Deutsch.

Barrett, S., and C. Fudge (1981). *Policy and Action.* London: Methuen.

Behn, R. D. (1978). How to Terminate a Public Policy: A Dozen Hints for a Would-be Terminator. *Policy Analysis* 4:393–413.

Benjamin, R. (1982). The Historical Nature of Social Science Knowledge: The Case of Comparative Political Inquiry. In E. Ostrom, ed., *Strategies of Political Inquiry.* Beverly Hills, Calif.: Sage.

Benjamin, R., and S. L. Elkin (1985). *The Democratic State.* Lawrence: University of Kansas Press.

Bennett, R. J. (1980). *The Geography of Public Finance.* London: Methuen.

Benson, J. K. (1975). The Intra-organization Network as Political Economy. *Administration Science Quarterly* 20:229–49.

Birnbaum, P. (1977). *Les sommets de l'état.* Paris: Editions du Seuil.

Blankart, C. B. (1980). Bureaucratic Problems in Public Choice. In K. W. Roskamp, ed., *Public Choice and Public Finance.* Paris: Editions Cujas.

Blau, P. M., and W. R. Scott (1962). *Formal Organizations.* San Francisco: Chandler.

Blumenthal, B. (1979). How Many People Really Work for the Federal Government? *National Journal* 11:703–13.

Bodiguel, J.-L. (1981). Conseils restreints, comités interministeriels, et réunions interministerielles. In F. de Baecque and J.-L. Quermonne, eds., *Administration et politique sous la Cinquième République.* Paris: Presses de la Fondation Nationale des Sciences Politiques.

——— (1984). High Level Officials in Eastern and Western European Countries: Problems Encountered in Comparative Research. In M. Niessen, J. Peschar, and C. Kourilsky, eds., *International Comparative Research.* Oxford: Pergamon.

Bonafede, D. (1979). A Day in the Life of a Cabinet Secretary. *National Journal* 11 (May 12):792–93.

Bowen, E. R. (1982). The Pressman-Wildavsky Paradox: Four Addenda or Why Models Based on Probability Theory Can Predict Implementation Success and Suggest Useful Tactical Advice for Implementors. *Journal of Public Policy* 2:1–22.

Braybrooke, D., and C. E. Lindblom (1963). *A Strategy of Decision.* New York: Free Press.

Breton, A., and R. Wintrobe (1975). The Equilibrium Size of a Budget-

Maximizing Bureau. *Journal of Political Economy* 83:195–207.

Bucovetsky, M. W. (1979). Governments as Indirect Employers. In M. W. Bucovetsky, ed., *Studies in Public Employment and Compensation in Canada*. Montreal: Butterworth.

Bunce, V. (1984). *Do New Leaders Make a Difference?* Princeton, N.J.: Princeton University Press.

Butler, S. M., M. Sanera, and W. B. Weinrod (1984). *Mandate for Leadership, II: Continuing the Conservative Revolution*. Washington, D.C.: Heritage Foundation.

Califano, J. A. (1981). *Governing America: An Insider's View*. New York: Simon and Schuster.

Campbell, C. (1983). *Governments under Stress*. Toronto: University of Toronto Press.

Campbell, C., and B. G. Peters (1988). Images of the Administrative Process: Politics, Administration, and Image IV. *Governance* 1, 80–101.

Campbell, C., and G. Szablowski (1979). *The Superbureaucrats: Structure and Behaviour in Central Agencies*. Toronto: Macmillan of Canada.

Campbell, D. T. (1975). "Degrees of Freedom" and the Case Study. *Comparative Political Studies* 8:178–93.

Campbell, D. T., and J. C. Stanley (1963). *Experimental and Quasi-experimental Designs for Research*. Chicago: Rand-McNally.

Carder, M., and B. Klingeberg (1980). Toward a Salaried Medical Profession. In A. J. Heidenheimer and N. Elvander, eds., *The Shaping of the Swedish Health System*. New York: St. Martin's.

Carroll, G. R., and J. Delacroix (1982). Organizational Mortality in the Newspaper Industries of Argentina and Ireland: An Ecological Approach. *Administrative Science Quarterly* 27:169–98.

Casstevens, T. W. (1984). Population Dynamics of Governmental Bureaus. *UMAP Journal* 5:178–99.

Castle, B. (1973). Mandarin Power. (London) *Sunday Times*, June 10.

Castles, F., and R. Wildemann (1986). *Visions and Realities of Party Government*. Amsterdam: DeGruyter.

Census of Canada (1971). Ottawa: Statistics Canada Statis Canada.

Chapman, R. (1978). *Your Disobedient Servant*. London: Chatto and Windus.

———— (1984). *Administrative Leadership*. London: Allen and Unwin.

Chester, D. W., and F. M. G. Willson (1968). *The Organization of British Central Administration, 1914–64*. 2d ed. London: Allen and Unwin.

Christoph, J. B. (1975). Higher Civil Servants and the Politics of Conservatism in Great Britain. In M. Dogan, ed., *The Mandarins of Western Europe*. New York: Wiley.

Cmnd. 9763-II (1986). *Statement on the Defence Estimates*. London: HMSO.

Cohen, M. D., J. G. March, and J. P. Olsen (1972). A Garbage Can Model of Organizational Choice. *Administrative Science Quarterly* 17:1–25.

Correa, H. (1979). A Quantitative Analysis of Public Administration and Government Efficiency. *Socio-Economic Planning Sciences* 13:256–63.

—— (1985). A Comparative Study of Bureaucratic Corruption in Latin America and the USA. *Socio-Economic Planning Sciences* 19:63–79.

Council of Civil Service Unions (1986). *Bulletin,* April:6, 56.

Cowart, A. (1978). The Economic Policies of European Governments. *British Journal of Political Science* 8:285–311, 425–39.

Crossman, R. (1975). *The Diaries of a Cabinet Minister, I.* London: Hamish Hamilton.

—— (1977). *The Diaries of a Cabinet Minister, II.* London: Hamish Hamilton.

Cyert, R. M., and J. G. March (1963). *A Behavioral Theory of the Firm.* Englewood Cliffs, N.J.: Prentice-Hall.

Dahl, R. A. (1957). The Concept of Power. *Behavioral Science* 2:201–15.

Darbel, A., and D. Schnapper (1969). *Les agents du système administratif.* Paris: Mouton.

—— (1972). *Le système administratif.* Paris: Mouton.

Davis, O. A., M. A. H. Dempster, and A. Wildavsky (1966). A Theory of the Budgetary Process. *American Political Science Review* 60:529–47.

—— (1974). Toward a Predictive Theory of the Federal Budgetary Process. *British Journal of Political Science* 4:419–52.

DeGrasse, R. W. (1983). *Military Expansion, Economic Decline.* Armonk, N.Y.: M. E. Sharpe.

DeLeon, P. (1978). Public Policy Termination: An End and a Beginning. *Policy Analysis* 4:369–92.

Derlien, H.-U. (1985). Politicization of the Civil Service in the Federal Republic of Germany: Facts and Fables. In F. Meyers, ed., *La politisation de l'administration.* Brussels: International Institute of Administrative Sciences.

Didot-Bottin (annual). *Bottin Administratif.* Paris: Didot-Bottin.

Dogan, M., ed. (1975). *The Mandarins of Western Europe.* New York: Wiley.

Doig, J. W. (1983). If I See a Murderous Fellow Sharpening a Knife Cleverly. *Public Administration Review* 43:292–304.

Downs, A. (1967). *Inside Bureaucracy.* Boston: Little, Brown.

Duffau, J.-M. (1983). Les rémunérations principales dans la fonction publique: Problématique générale. *Revue française d'administration publique* 28:75–87.

Dunn, W. N., and E. Ginzberg (forthcoming). A Socio-cognitive Approach to Organizational Analysis. *Human Relations.*

Dunn, W. N., and F. W. Swierczek (1977). Planned Organizational Change: Toward Grounded Theory. *Journal of Applied Behavioral Science* 13:135–57.

Dye, T. R. (1966). *Politics, Economics, and the Public.* Chicago: Rand-McNally.

Dyson, K. H. F. (1980). *The State Tradition in Western Europe.* Oxford: Martin Robertson.

Eisenstadt, S. N. (1963). *The Political Systems of Empires.* New York: Free Press.

Eldersveld, S. J. (1965). Bureaucratic Contact with the Public in India. *Indian Journal of Political Science* 11:221–33.

Eldersveld, S. J., S. Hubee-Boonzaijer, and J. Kooiman (1975). Elite Perceptions of the Political Process in the Netherlands. In M. Dogan, ed., *The Mandarins of Western Europe.* New York: Wiley.

Eldersveld, S. J., V. Jagannadham, and A. P. Barnabas (1968). *The Citizen and the Administrator in a Developing Democracy.* Glenview, Ill.: Scott, Foresman.

Eldersveld, S. J., J. Kooiman, and T. van der Tak (1981). *Elite Images in Dutch Politics.* Ann Arbor: University of Michigan Press.

Employment and Training Administration. See U.S. Department of Labor (annual).

Esman, M. J. (1966). The Politics of Development Administration. In J. D. Montgomery and W. J. Siffin, eds., *Approaches to Development: Politics, Administration and Change.* New York: McGraw-Hill.

FDA News (monthly). London: Association of First Division Civil Servants.

Feigenbaum, H. G. (1985). *The Politics of Public Enterprise: Oil and the French State.* Princeton, N. J.: Princeton University Press.

Ferriman, A., and C. Wolmar (1986). A Tale of Two Systems. *Observer,* May 18.

Fiorina, M. P. (1977). *Congress: Keystone of the Washington Establishment.* New Haven, Conn.: Yale University Press.

Fivelsdal, E., T. B. Jørgensen, and P.-E. D. Jensen (1979). *Interessorganisationer og Centraladministration.* Copenhagen: Nyt fra Samfundsvidenskaberne.

Flora, P., and A. J. Heidenheimer (1981). *The Development of the Welfare State in Europe and America.* New Brunswick, N.J.: Transaction.

Foot, D. K. (1979). *Public Employment in Canada: Statistical Series.* Toronto: Butterworth.

Frederickson, H. G. (1980). *The New Public Administration.* University: University of Alabama Press.

Freeman, J. H., G. R. Carroll, and M. T. Hannan (1983). The Liability of Newness: Age Dependence in Organizational Death Rates.

American Sociological Review 48:692–710.

Freeman, J. H., and M. Hannan (1983). Niche Width and the Dynamics of Organizational Populations. *American Journal of Sociology* 88:1116–45.

Freeman, J. L. (1965). *The Political Process.* New York: Random House.

Fried, R. (1967). *The Italian Prefects.* New Haven, Conn.: Yale University Press.

Garrett, J. (1980). *Managing the Civil Service.* London: Heinemann.

Gboyega, A. (1984). The Federal Character; or, the Attempt to Create Representative Bureaucracies in Nigeria. *International Review of Administrative Sciences* 50:17–24.

Gershuny, J. I. (1978). *After Industrial Society: The Emerging Self-Service Economy.* London: Macmillan.

Ginzberg, E. (1976). The Pluralistic Economy of the United States. *Scientific American*, December: 25–29.

Gist, J. R. (1977). "Increment" and "Base" in the Congressional Appropriations Process. *American Journal of Political Science* 21:341–52.

Gladden, E. N. (1972). *A History of Public Administration.* 2 vols. London: Frank Cass.

Good, D. A. (1980). *The Politics of Anticipation: Making Canadian Tax Policy.* Ottawa: Carleton University, School of Public Administration.

Goodin, R. E. (1982). Rational Politicians and Rational Bureaucrats in Washington and Whitehall. *Public Administration* 60:23–41.

——— (1983). *Political Theory and Public Policy.* Chicago: University of Chicago Press.

Goodsell, C. T. (1976). Cross-Cultural Comparison of Behavior of Postal Clerks toward Clients. *Administrative Science Quarterly* 21:140–50.

——— (1981). *The Public Encounter.* Bloomington: University of Indiana Press.

——— (1984). O contato com o publico no tercerio mundo. *Revista de Administração Pública* 18:48–65.

——— (1985). *The Case for Bureaucracy.* 2d ed. Chatham, N.J.: Chatham House.

Gordon, M. R. (1971). Civil Servants, Politicians, and Parties: Shortcomings in the British Policy Press. *Comparative Politics* 4:29–58.

Gormley, W. (1983). *The Politics of Public Utility Regulation.* Pittsburgh: University of Pittsburgh Press.

Gough, I. (1979). *The Political Economy of the Welfare State.* London: Macmillan.

Gournay, B. (1984). The Higher Civil Service of France. In B. L. R. Smith, ed., *The Higher Civil Service in Europe and Canada.* Washington, D.C.: Brookings Institution.

Grafton, C. (1984). Response to Change: The Creation and Reorganization of Federal Agencies. In R. Miewald and M. Steinman, eds., *Problems of Administrative Reform*. Chicago: Nelson-Hall.

Gray, A., and W. I. Jenkins (1985). *Administrative Politics in British Government*. Brighton, Sussex: Wheatsheaf.

Greenstein, F. I. (1982). *The Hidden Hand Presidency: Eisenhower as Leader*. New York: Basic Books.

Greenwood, R., and C. R. Hinings (1976). Contingency Theories and Public Bureaucracies. *Policy and Politics* 5:159–80.

Greenwood, R., C. R. Hinings, and S. Ranson (1975a). Contingency Theory and the Organization of Local Authorities I: Differentiation and Integration. *Public Administration* 53:1–23.

––––––– (1975b). Contingency Theory and the Organization of Local Authorities II: Contingencies and Structures. *Public Administration* 53:169–90.

Gremion, C. (1979). *Profession: Décideurs: Pouvoir des hauts fonctionnaires et réforme de l'état*. Paris: Gauthier-Villars.

Grindle, M. S. (1980). *Politics and Policy Implementation in the Third World*. Princeton, N.J.: Princeton University Press.

Gulick, L., and L. Urwick (1937). *Papers on the Science of Administration*. New York: Institute of Public Administration.

Guttman, P. M. (1977). The Subterranean Economy. *Financial Analyst's Journal* 33:26–27.

Hague, D. C., and B. L. R. Smith (1971). *The Dilemma of Accountability in Modern Government*. London: Macmillan.

Haire, M., E. E. Ghiselli, and L. W. Porter (1966). *Managerial Thinking: An International Study*. New York: Wiley.

Halász, J. (1985). A Comparative Study of Socialist Public Administration. In G. Szoboszlai, ed., *Politics and Public Administration in Hungary*. Budapest: Akadémiai Kiadó.

Ham, C., and M. Hill (1984). *The Policy Process in the Modern Capitalist State*. Brighton, Sussex: Wheatsheaf.

Hancock, D. M. (1983). Comparative Public Policy. In A. Finifter, ed., *Political Science: The State of the Discipline*. Washington, D.C.: American Political Science Association.

Hanf, K., and F. W. Scharpf (1978). *Interorganizational Policymaking: Limits to Coordination and Central Control*. Beverly Hills, Calif.: Sage.

Hannan, M., and J. H. Freeman (1977). The Population Ecology Model of Organizations. *American Journal of Sociology* 82:929–64.

Hanusch, H., ed. (1983). *Anatomy of Government Deficiencies*. Berlin: Springer.

Harmon, M. M. (1981). *Action Theory for Public Administration*. New York: Longman.

Hautphenne, P. (1966). *Les associations des communes en Belgique*.

Brussels: Unions des Villes et Communes Belges.

Hawker, G. (1981). *Who's Master, Who's Servant? Reforming Bureaucracy.* Sydney: Allen and Unwin.

Headey, B. (1974). *British Cabinet Ministers.* London: Allen and Unwin.

Heady, F. (1979). *Public Administration: A Comparative Perspective.* New York: Dekker.

Heald, D. (1983). *Public Expenditure: Its Defence and Reform.* Oxford: Martin Robertson.

Heclo, H. (1974). *Modern Social Politics in Britain and Sweden.* New Haven, Conn.: Yale University Press.

—————— (1977). *A Government of Strangers.* Washington, D.C.: Brookings Institution.

—————— (1978). Issue Networks and the Executive Establishment. In A. King, ed., *The New American Political System.* Washington, D.C.: American Enterprise Institute.

—————— (1984). A Comment on the Future of the U.S. Civil Service. In Bruce L. R. Smith, ed., *The Higher Civil Service in Europe and Canada: Lessons for the United States.* Washington, D.C.: Brookings Institution.

Heclo, H., and A. Wildavsky (1974). *The Private Government of Public Money.* Berkeley: University of California Press.

Heidenheimer, A. J., H. Heclo, and C. T. Adams (1984). *Comparative Public Policy.* 2d ed. New York: St. Martin's.

Heller, P. S., and A. A. Tait (1983). *Government Employment and Pay: Some International Comparisons.* Washington, D.C.: International Monetary Fund.

Herrmann, M. L., J. Langkau, R. Weinert, and R. Nejedlo (1983). *Frauen in öffentlichen Dienst.* Bonn: Neue Gesellschaft.

Hjern, B., and C. Hull (1982). Implementation Research as Empirical Constitutionalism. *European Journal of Political Research* 10:105–15.

Hjern, B., and D. Porter (1981). Implementation Structures: A New Unit of Administrative Analysis. *Organization Studies* 2:211–24.

Hoetjes, B. J. S. (1977). *Corruptie in Ontwikkelingslanded.* Leiden: Martinus Nijhoff.

Hofferbert, R. (1966). The Relationship between Public Policy and Some Structural and Environmental Variables in the American States. *American Political Science Review* 60:73–82.

Hogwood, B. W., and B. G. Peters (1983). *Policy Dynamics.* Brighton, Sussex: Wheatsheaf.

—————— (1985). *The Pathology of Public Policy.* New York: Oxford University Press.

Holland, P. (1981). *The Government of Quangos.* London: Adam Smith Institute.

Hood, C. (1976). *The Limits of Administration*. New York: Wiley.

———— (1986). *The Tools of Government*. Chatham, N.J.: Chatham House.

Hood, C., and A. Dunsire (1981). *Bureaumetrics*. Farnsborough, Hants.: Gower.

Hood, C., M. Huby, and A. Dunsire (1984). Do British Central Government Departments Measure Up to the Budget/Utility Theory of Bureaucracy? *Journal of Public Policy* 4:163–79.

Hoskyns, J. (1983). Whitehall and Westminster: An Outsider's View. *Fiscal Studies* 3:162–72.

Hunter, F. (1953). *Community Power Structure: A Study of Decision-Makers*. Chapel Hill: University of North Carolina Press.

Ingraham, P. W., and C. Ban (1986). Models of Public Management: Are They Useful to Federal Workers in the 1980s? *Public Administration Review* 46:152–60.

Institute of Directors (1986). *Reskilling Government*. London: Institute of Directors.

Jackson, P. M. (1982). *The Political Economy of Bureaucracy*. Oxford: Philip Allan.

Johansen, L. N., and O. P. Kristensen (1982). Corporatist Traits in Denmark, 1946–76. In G. Lehmbruch and P. Schmitter, eds., *Patterns of Corporatist Policy-Making*. Beverly Hills, Calif.: Sage.

Jones, G. W. (1985). The Prime Minister's Advisers. In A. King, ed., *The British Prime Minister*. Durham, N.C.: Duke University Press.

Jordan, A. G. (1981). Iron Triangles, Woolly Corporatism, or Elastic Nets: Images of the Policy Process. *Journal of Public Policy* 1:95–124.

Jun, J. (1976). Renewing the Study of Comparative Administration: Some Reflections on Current Possibilities. *Public Administration Review* 36:641–47.

Katz, D., and R. L. Kahn (1978). *The Social Psychology of Organizations*. New York: Wiley.

Katz, E., and S. N. Eisenstadt (1960). Some Sociological Observations on the Response of Israeli Organizations to New Immigrants. *Administrative Science Quarterly* 5:113–33.

Katz, E., B. A. Gutek, R. L. Kahn, and E. Barton (1975). *Bureaucratic Encounters*. Ann Arbor: University of Michigan, Institute for Social Research.

Kaufman, H. (1976). *Are Government Organizations Immortal?* Washington, D.C.: Brookings Institution.

———— (1981a). The Fear of Bureaucracy: A Raging Pandemic. *Public Administration Review* 41:1–9.

———— (1981b). *The Administrative Behavior of Federal Bureau Chiefs*. Washington, D.C.: Brookings Institution.

———— (1985). *Time, Chance, and Organizations*. Chatham, N.J.: Chatham House.

Kaufmann, F. X. (1977). *Bürgernahe Gestaltung der sozialen Umwelt.* Meisenheim: Anton Hain.

Kellner, P., and Lord Crowther-Hunt (1980). *The Civil Service: An Inquiry into Britain's Ruling Class.* London: Macdonald.

Kingsley, J. D. (1944). *Representative Bureaucracy.* Yellow Springs, Ohio: Antioch Press.

Klein, R. (1983). *The Politics of the National Health Service.* London: Longman.

Klein, R., and J. Lewis (1977). Advice and Dissent in British Government: The Case of Special Advisers. *Policy and Politics* 6:1–25.

Klingman, D. (1980). Temporal and Spatial Diffusion in Comparative Analysis of Social Change. *American Political Science Review* 74:123–37.

Kogan, M. (1973). *Comment on Niskanen's "Bureaucracy: Servant or Master?"* London: Institute of Economic Affairs.

Kornberg, A. (1973). *Legislatures in Comparative Perspective.* New York: McKay.

Krislov, S., and D. H. Rosenbloom (1981). *Representative Bureaucracy and the American Political System.* New York: Praeger.

Kvavik, R. B. (1978). *Interest Groups in Norwegian Politics.* Oslo: Universitetsforlaget.

Laegreid, R., and J. P. Olsen (1978). *Byråkrati og Beslutningar.* Oslo: Universitetsforlaget.

Lane, J. E., ed. (1985). *State and Market: The Politics of the Public and the Private.* London: Sage.

LaPalombara, J. (1963). *Bureaucracy and Political Development.* Princeton, N.J.: Princeton University Press.

Lasswell, H. D., and A. Kaplan (1950). *Power and Society.* New Haven, Conn.: Yale University Press.

Lawrence, P. R., and J. W. Lorsch (1967). *Organization and Environment.* Homewood, Ill: Irwin.

Leemans, A. F. (1976). *Management of Change in Government.* The Hague: Martinus Nijhoff.

Lehner, F. (1985). Modes of Interest Intermediation and the Structure of Political Power: An Investigation into Political Efficacy. Paper presented at the Thirteenth World Congress of the International Political Science Association, Paris, July.

Leichter, H. M. (1979). *A Comparative Approach to Policy Analysis.* Cambridge: Cambridge University Press.

Lewis, A. (1982). *The Psychology of Taxation.* Oxford: Martin Robertson.

Lindbeck, A. (1974). *Swedish Economic Policy.* Berkeley, Calif: University of California Press.

Linder, S. H., and B. G. Peters (1985). From Social Theory to Policy Design. *Journal of Public Policy* 4:237–59.

—— (forthcoming). Implementation Research: The Fallacy of Misplaced Precision. *Policy Studies Review.*

Lipset, S. M. (1963). *The First New Nation: The United States in Historical and Comparative Perspective.* New York: Basic Books.

Lipsky, M. (1980). *Street-Level Bureaucracy: Dilemmas of the Individual in Public Services.* New York: Russell Sage Foundation.

Long, N. (1962). Power and Administration. In N. Long, ed., *The Polity.* Chicago: Rand-McNally.

Lord, G. (1973). *The French Budgetary Process.* Berkeley: University of California Press.

Lundquist, L. (1985). From Order to Chaos: Recent Trends in the Study of Public Administration. In J. E. Lane, ed., *State and Market: The Politics of the Public and the Private.* London: Sage.

Lundquist, L., and K. Ståhlberg (1983). *Byråkrati i Norden.* Åbo, Finland: Åbo Akademi.

Lynn, J., and A. Jay (1982). *Yes, Minister.* Vol. 2. London: British Broadcasting Corporation.

Lynn, L. E. (1981). *Managing the Public's Business.* New York: Basic Books.

Machin, H. (1977). *The Prefect in French Public Administration.* London: Croom-Helm.

McKelvey, B. (1982). *Organizational Systematics: Taxonomy, Evolution, Classification.* Berkeley: University of California Press.

McKelvey, B., and H. Aldrich (1983). Populations, Natural Selection, and Applied Organizational Science. *Administrative Science Quarterly* 28:101–28.

Malek, F. V. (1978). *Washington's Hidden Tragedy: The Failure to Make Government Work.* New York: Free Press.

March, J. G., and J. P. Olsen (1983). What Administrative Reorganization Tells Us about Governing. *American Political Science Review* 77:281–96.

———— (1984). The New Institutionalism: Organizational Factors in Political Life. *American Political Science Review* 78:734–49.

Marinen, O. (1980). Law Enforcement and Political Change in Post–Civil War Nigeria. Paper presented at the annual meeting of the American Society for Public Administration, New York, April.

Marris, R. (1964). *The Economics of Managerial Capitalism.* New York: Free Press.

Martin, J. P. (1982). Public Sector Employment Trends. In *Public Finance and Public Employment.* Detroit: Wayne State University Press.

Mashaw, J. L. (1983). *Bureaucratic Justice.* New Haven, Conn.: Yale University Press.

Mayhew, D. R. (1974). *Congress: The Electoral Connection.* New Haven, Conn.: Yale University Press.

Mayntz, R., ed. (1980). *Implementation politischer Programme.* Konigstein: Verlagsgruppe Athenäum.

Mayntz, R. (1984). The Higher Civil Service of the Federal Republic of Germany. In B. L. R. Smith, ed., *The Higher Civil Service in Europe and Canada*. Washington, D.C.: Brookings Institution.

——— (1985). German Federal Bureaucrats: A Functional Elite between Politics and Administration. In E. N. Suleiman, ed., *Bureaucrats and Policymaking*. New York: Holmes and Meier.

Meier, K. (1975). Representative Bureaucracy: An Empirical Assessment. *American Political Science Review* 69:526–42.

Mellbourn, A. (1979). *Byråkratins Ansikten*. Stockholm: Liber.

Merton, R. (1940). Bureaucratic Structure and Personality. *Social Forces* 18:560–68.

Meyer, M. W., W. Stevenson, and S. Webster (1984). *Limits to Bureaucratic Growth*. Hawthorne, N.Y.: Aldine.

Meyers, F. (1985). *La politisation de l'administration*. Brussels: International Institute of Administrative Sciences.

Migue, J.-L., and G. Belanger (1974). Toward a General Theory of Managerial Discretion. *Public Choice* 17:27–43.

Moe, R. (1980). *The Federal Executive Establishment: Evolution and Trends*. Washington, D.C.: Government Printing Office.

Moe, T. (1984). The New Economics of Organizations. *American Journal of Political Science* 28:739–77.

Mohr, L. B. (1973). The Concept of Organizational Goal. *American Political Science Review* 67:470–81.

Molitor, A. (1983). L'histoire de l'administration: Introduction. *International Review of Administrative Sciences* 49:1–3.

Morgenthau, H. J. (1948). *Politics among Nations*. New York: Knopf.

Mosher, F. C. (1978). Professions in the Public Service. *Public Administration Review* 38:144–50.

——— (1979). *The GAO: The Quest for Accountability in American Government*. Boulder, Colo.: Westview.

——— (1980). The Changing Responsibilities and Tactics of the Federal Government. *Public Administration Review* 40:541–48.

Muramatsu, M., and E. S. Krauss (1984). Bureaucrats and Politicians in Policymaking: The Case of Japan. *American Political Science Review* 78:126–46.

Murphy, T. P., D. E. Nuechterlein, and R. J. Stupak (1978). *Inside the Bureaucracy: The View from the Assistant Secretary's Desk*. Boulder, Colo.: Westview.

Musolf, A., and H. Seidman (1980). The Blurred Boundaries of Public Administration. *Public Administration Review* 40:124–30.

Nachmias, D., and D. H. Rosenbloom (1978). *Bureaucratic Culture: Citizens and Administrators in Israel*. New York: St. Martin's.

Nakamura, R. T., and F. Smallwood (1980). *The Politics of Policy Implementation*. New York: St. Martin's.

Natchez, P. B., and I. C. Bupp (1973). Policy and Priority in the Budgetary Process. *American Political Science Review* 67:951–63.

Nathan, R. P. (1975). *The Plot that Failed: Nixon and the Administrative Presidency.* New York: Wiley.

Neustadt, R. E. (1973). Politicians and Bureaucrats. In T. D. Truman, ed., *American Assembly, Congress, and America's Future.* Englewood Cliffs, N.J.: Prentice-Hall.

Newton, K. (1978). Is Small So Beautiful? Is Big So Ugly? *Studies in Public Policy,* no. 18:(Glasgow, Scotland: Centre for the Study of Public Policy, University of Strathclyde.)

Niskanen, W. (1971). *Bureaucracy and Representative Government.* Chicago: Aldine/Atherton.

Nystrom, P., and W. Starbuck (1981). *Handbook of Organizational Design.* New York: Oxford University Press.

Office of Management and Budget (annual-a). *Budget of the United States Government.* Washington, D.C.: Government Printing Office.

———— (annual-b). *Budget of the United States, Special Analyses.* Washington, D.C.: Government Printing Office.

Office of Personnel Management (annual). *Annual Report.* Washington, D.C.: Government Printing Office.

———— (biennial). *Occupations of Federal White-Collar Workers.* Washington, D.C.: Office of Personnel Management.

Office of the Federal Register (1982). *The United States Government Manual, 1982/83.* Washington, D.C.: Government Printing Office.

———— (1984). *The United States Government Manual, 1984/85.* Washington, D.C.: Government Printing Office.

Olsen, J. P. (1983). *Organized Democracy.* Oslo: Universitetsforlaget.

Orzechowski, W. (1977). Economic Models of Bureaucracy: Survey, Extensions, and Evidence. In T. E. Borcherding, ed., *Budgets and Bureaucrats: The Sources of Government Growth.* Durham, N.C.: Duke University Press.

Ouchi, W. (1981). *Theory Z: How American Business Can Meet the Japanese Challenge.* Reading, Mass.: Addison-Wesley.

Page, E. C. (1985). *Political Authority and Bureaucratic Power.* Brighton, Sussex: Wheatsheaf.

Parris, H. (1969). *Constitutional Bureaucracy.* London: Allen and Unwin.

Peacock, A. T. (1979). *The Economic Analysis of Government and Related Themes.* Oxford: Martin Robertson.

———— (1983). Public X-Inefficiency: Informational and Institutional Constraints. In H. Hanusch, ed., *Anatomy of Government Deficiencies.* Berlin: Springer.

Peters, B. G. (1972). Political and Economic Effects on the Development of Social Expenditures in France, Sweden, and the United Kingdom. *Midwest Journal of Political Science* 16:225–38.

———— (1981). The Problem of Bureaucratic Government. *Journal of Politics* 43:56–82.

———— (1984). *The Politics of Bureaucracy.* 2d ed. New York: Longman.

———— (1985a). The Structure and Organization of Government: Concepts and Issues. *Journal of Public Policy* 5:107–20.

———— (1985b). The United States: Absolute Change and Relative Stability. In R. Rose et al., eds., *Public Employment in Western Nations.* Cambridge: Cambridge University Press.

———— (1985c). Sweden: The Explosion of Public Employment. In R. Rose et al., eds., *Public Employment in Western Nations.* Cambridge: Cambridge University Press.

———— (1986a). The Relationship between Civil Servants and Political Executives: A Preliminary Comparative Inquiry. In J. E. Lane, ed., *Bureaucracy and Public Choice.* London: Sage.

———— (1986b). Burning the Village: The Civil Service under Reagan and Thatcher. *Parliamentary Affairs* 39:79–97.

———— (1986c). Providing Public Services: The Public and Private Employment Mix. In D. L. Thompson, ed., *The Private Exercise of Public Functions.* Lexington, Mass.: Lexington Books.

Peters, B. G., and M. O. Heisler (1983). Thinking about Public Sector Growth. In C. L. Taylor, ed., *Why Governments Grow: Measuring Public Sector Size.* Beverly Hills, Calif.: Sage.

Peters, B. G., and B. W. Hogwood (1985). Up and Down with the Issue-Attention Cycle. *Journal of Politics* 47:238–53.

———— (forthcoming). *The Changing Face of the Washington Bureaucracy.*

Pierce, W. S. (1981). *Bureaucratic Failure and Public Expenditure.* New York: Academic Press.

Pignatelli, A. C. (1985). Italy: The Development of a Late Developing State. In R. Rose et al., *Public Employment in Western Nations.* Cambridge: Cambridge University Press.

Pitt, D. C., and B. C. Smith (1981). *Government Departments: An Organizational Perspective.* London: Routledge and Kegan Paul.

Pliatzky, L. (1982). *Getting and Spending.* Oxford: Basil Blackwell.

Pollitt, C. (1984). *Manipulating the Machine: Changing the Pattern of Ministerial Departments, 1960–83.* London: Allen and Unwin.

Polsby, N. W. (1984). *Political Innovation in America: The Politics of Policy Innovation.* New Haven, Conn.: Yale University Press.

Pommerehne, W., and B. S. Frey (1978). Bureaucratic Behavior in Democracy: A Case Study. *Public Finance* 33:98–112.

Porter, R. B. (1980). *Presidential Decision-Making: The Economic Policy Board.* London: Cambridge University Press.

President's Private Sector Survey on Cost Control (1984). *Report to the President.* Washington, D.C.: Government Printing Office.

Pressman, J. L., and A. Wildavsky (1973). *Implementation.* Berkeley: University of California Press.

Prottas, J. M. (1979). *People Processing: The Street Level Bureaucrat in*

Public Service Bureaucracies. Lexington, Mass.: Lexington Books.

Pryor, F. (1968). *Public Expenditures in Communist and Capitalist Nations.* Homewood, Ill.: Irwin.

Putnam, R. D. (1973). The Political Attitudes of Senior Civil Servants in Western Europe: A Preliminary Report. *British Journal of Political Science* 3:257–90.

—— (1976). *The Comparative Study of Political Elites.* Englewood Cliffs, N.J.: Prentice-Hall.

Pye, L. (1962). *Politics, Personality, and Nation-building.* New Haven, Conn.: Yale University Press.

Quah, J. S. T. (1982). Tackling Bureaucratic Corruption: The ASEAN Experience. In G. E. Caiden and H. Siedentopf, eds., *Strategies for Administrative Reform.* Lexington, Mass.: Lexington Books.

Redwood, J. (1984). *Going for Broke: Gambling with the Taxpayer's Money.* Oxford: Basil Blackwell.

Rein, M. (1985). Social Policy and Labor Markets: The Employment Role of Social Provision. Paper presented at the Thirteenth World Congress of the International Political Science Association, Paris, July.

—— (1986). Spesa dello stato sociale e occupazione. *Biblioteca della Libertà* 93:83–116.

Richardson, J. (1982). *Policy Styles in Western Europe.* London: Allen and Unwin.

Richardson, S. A. (1956). Organizational Contrasts on British and American Ships. *Administrative Science Quarterly* 1:189–207.

Ridley, F. F. (1979). *Government and Administration in Western Europe.* Oxford: Martin Robertson.

Riggs, F. W. (1964). *Administration in Developing Countries: The Theory of Prismatic Society.* Boston: Houghton Mifflin.

—— (1976). The Group and the Movement: Notes on Comparative Development Administration. *Public Administration Review* 36:641–45.

Roethlisberger, F. J., and W. J. Dickson (1939). *Management and the Worker.* Cambridge, Mass.: Harvard University Press.

Roos, L. L., and N. P. Roos (1971). *Managers of Modernization.* Cambridge, Mass.: Harvard University Press.

Rose, R. (1974). *The Problem of Party Government.* London: Macmillan.

—— (1976). On the Priorities of Government. *European Journal of Political Research* 4:247–89.

—— (1980). Government against Subgovernments: A European Perspective on Washington. In R. Rose and E. N. Suleiman, eds., *Presidents and Prime Ministers.* Washington, D.C.: American Enterprise Institute.

—— (1985a). *Understanding Big Government.* London: Sage.

—— (1985b). Getting By in Three Economies. In J. E. Lane, ed., *State and Market: The Politics of the Public and the Private.* London: Sage.

Rose, R., and E. N. Suleiman, eds. (1980). *Presidents and Prime Ministers.* Washington, D.C.: American Enterprise Institute.

Rose, R., E. Page, R. Parry, B. G. Peters, A. Pignatelli, and K. D. Schmidt (1985). *Public Employment in Western Nations.* Cambridge: Cambridge University Press.

Rothman, S., and S. R. Lichter (1983). How Liberal Are Bureaucrats? *Regulation* 7:16–32.

Rourke, F. E. (1979). Bureaucratic Autonomy and the Public Interest. *American Behavioral Scientist* 22:537–46.

Rowan, H. (1979). Kreps' Introspective Farewell. *Washington Post,* November 3.

Rowat, D. C., ed. (1984). *Global Comparisons in Public Administration.* Ottawa: Carleton University.

Salamon, L. (1981a). Rethinking Public Management: Third-Party Government and the Changing Forms of Government Action. *Public Policy* 29:255–75.

——— (1981b). The Question of Goals. In P. Szanton, ed., *Federal Reorganization: What Have We Learned?* Chatham, N.J.: Chatham House, 58–84.

Savage, P. (1976). Optimism and Pessimism in Comparative Administration. *Public Administration Review* 36:415–23.

Savas, E. S. (1979). *Privatizing the Public Sector.* Chatham, N.J.: Chatham House.

Schmitter, P. C., and G. Lehmbruch (1982). *Trends toward Corporatist Intermediation.* London: Sage.

Seidman, H., and R. Gilmour (1986). *Politics, Power, and Position.* New York: Oxford University Press.

Self, P. (1972). *Administrative Theories and Politics.* London: George Allen and Unwin.

Sharkansky, I. (1967). *Spending in the American States.* Chicago: Rand-McNally.

——— (1979). *Wither the State?* Chatham, N.J.: Chatham House.

Siffin, W. J. (1971). Bureaucracy: The Problem of Methodology and the "Structural Approach." *Journal of Comparative Administration* 2:471–503.

Sigelman, L. (1986) The Bureaucrat as Budget Maximizer: An Assumption Examined. *Public Budgeting and Finance* 6:50–59.

Simon, H. A. (1947). *Administrative Behavior.* New York: Macmillan.

Simon, H. A., D. W. Smithburg, and V. A. Thompson (1950). *Public Administration.* New York: Knopf.

Sjoberg, G., R. A. Brymer, and B. Farris (1978). Bureaucracy and the Lower Class. In F. Rourke, ed., Bureaucratic Power in National Politics. 3d ed. Boston: Little, Brown.

Spann, R. M. (1977). Public and Private Provision of Government Services. In T. E. Borcherding, ed., *Budgets and Bureaucrats*. Durham, N.C.: Duke University Press.

Stahl, I. (1976). En ekonomisk teori for blandekonomi. In *Erfarenheter av Blandekonomin*. Stockholm: Skandinaviska Enskilda Banken.

Ståhlberg, K. (1985). The Politicization of Public Administration. Paper presented at the annual meeting of the European Group on Public Administration, Leuven, Belgium.

Stanbury, W. T. (1980). *Government Regulation: Scope, Growth, Process*. Montreal: Institute for Research on Public Policy.

Standard and Poor (1985). *Corporate Reports*. New York: Standard and Poor.

Statistiska Centralbyrån (annual). *Arbetsmarknadsstatistisk Årsbok*. Stockholm: Statistiska Centralbyrån.

———— (1980). *Folkrakningen*. Stockholm: Statistiska Centralbyrån.

Steinkemper, B. (1974). *Klassische und politische Bürokraten in der Ministerialverwaltung der Bundesrepublik Deutschland*. Cologne: Carl Heymanns.

Stern, I. (1975). Industry Effects of Government Expenditures: An Input-Output Analysis. *Survey of Current Business* 55:9–23.

Stevens, A. (1985). *L'Alternance* and the Higher Civil Service. In P. G. Cerny and M. A. Schain, eds., *Socialism, the State, and Public Policy in France*. London: Frances Pinter.

Stone, D. (1980). *The Limits of Professional Power*. Chicago: University of Chicago Press.

Suleiman, E. N. (1974). *Politics, Power, and Bureaucracy in France: The Administrative Elite*. Princeton, N.J.: Princeton University Press.

———— (1978). *Elites in French Society*. Princeton, N.J.: Princeton University Press.

———— (1985). Bureaucrats, Politics, and Policy Making in France. In E. N. Suleiman, ed., *Bureaucrats and Policymaking*. New York: Holmes and Meier.

Sveriges Statskalendar (annual). Stockholm: Liberforlag.

Szablowski, G. (1981). Executive-Bureaucratic Politics. Paper presented at the annual meeting of the Midwest Political Science Association.

Tarschys, D. (1973). *Petita: Hur Svenska myndigheter argumentar för högre anslag*. Stockholm: Publica.

———— (1977). The Problem of the Pre-planned Society. Paper presented at the annual meeting of the American Political Science Association, Washington, D.C., September.

———— (1985). Curbing Public Expenditure: Current Trends. *Journal of Public Policy* 5:23–67.

Tullock, G. (1965). *The Politics of Bureaucracy*. Washington, D.C.: Public Affairs Press.

_____ (1974). Dynamic Hypothesis on Bureaucracy. *Public Choice* 19:127:31.

Tummala, K. K. (1982). *Administrative Systems Abroad.* Washington, D.C.: University Press of America.

Udy, S. (1959). The Structure of Authority in Non-Industrial Production Organizations. *American Journal of Sociology* 64:582–84.

U.S. Bureau of the Census (1969). *Census of Governments, 1967.* Washington, D.C.: Government Printing Office.

_____ (1974). *Census of Governments, 1972.* Washington, D.C.: Government Printing Office.

_____ (1982). *Census of Governments, 1980.* Washington, D.C.: Government Printing Office.

_____ (annual-a). *Report of the President's Pay Agent.* Washington, D.C.: Government Printing Office.

_____ (annual-b). *Statistical Abstract of the United States.* Washington, D.C.: Government Printing Office.

U.S. Department of Defense (annual). *Defense Manpower Statistics.* Washington, D.C.: Department of Defense.

U.S. Department of Defense, Division of Information, Operations, and Reports (1985). *Top 100 Corporations.* Washington, D.C.: Department of Defense.

U.S. Department of Labor, Employment and Training Administration (annual). *Annual Report to the President.* Washington, D.C.: Government Printing Office.

Van der Wielen, H. (1983). The Public Sector's Interaction with the Market Sector: The Netherlands. In C. L. Taylor, ed., *Why Governments Grow: Measuring Public Sector Size.* Beverly Hills, Calif.: Sage.

Vernon, R. (1984). Linking Managers with Ministers: Dilemmas of the State-Owned Enterprise. *Journal of Policy Analysis and Management* 4:39–55.

Vinde, P., and G. Petri (1975). *Hur Sveriges Styres.* Stockholm: Prisma.

Waara, L. (1980). *Den Statliga Företagssektorns Expansion.* Stockholm: Liber.

Walsh, A. H. (1978). *The Public's Business.* Cambridge, Mass.: MIT Press.

Washington Post (1981). Education Secretary Bell Recommends Abolition of U.S. Department of Education. August 7.

Webb, E. J., D. T. Campbell, R. D. Schwartz, and L. Sechrest (1966). *Unobtrusive Measures.* Chicago: Rand-McNally.

Wheare, K. C. (1973). *Maladministration and Its Remedies.* London: Stevens.

White, O. F. (1969). The Dialectical Organization: An Alternative to Bureaucracy. *Public Administration Review* 39:32–42.

Wildavsky, A. (1984). *The Politics of the Budgetary Process.* 4th ed.

References

Boston: Little, Brown.

Wilson, W. (1887). The Study of Administration. *Political Science Quarterly* 2:209–13.

Wittfogel, K. A. (1957). *Oriental Despotism.* New Haven, Conn.: Yale University Press.

Wolf, C. (1979). A Theory of Non-market Failure: Framework for Implementation Analysis. *Journal of Law and Economics* 26:107–40.

Wollmann, H. (1980). Implementationsforschung–Eine Chance für kritische Verwaltungsforschung. In H. Wollmann, ed., *Politik im Dickicht der Bürokratie.* Oplanden: Westdeutscher.

Wright, M. (1980). Ministers and Civil Servants: Relations and Responsibilities. *Parliamentary Affairs* 33:293–313.

Young, H., and A. Sloman (1982). *No, Minister.* London: British Broadcasting Corporation.

———— (1984). *But, Chancellor.* London: British Broadcasting Corporation.

Index

209

Index

Index

Index

Privatization, 44, 51
Professionalism, 7, 15, 29–30, 37
Prottas, J. M., 20, 110, 111, 203
Pryor, F., 23, 204
Public choice, 119–23
Public employees, 14, 15, 22, 24, 26–60
Public employment, 28, 40–55, 136–37, 183–84
  indirect, 53–55
  mixture with private, 17, 40–52, 77, 184
  part-time, 28
  women, 28–29, 34
Public expenditures, 11–12
Public sector pay, 14–15, 37–39, 129, 133–36, 158, 166
Public sector pensions, 37, 136
Putnam, R. D., 9, 15, 16, 21, 34, 36, 148, 150, 185, 190, 204
Pye, L., 115, 204

Quah, J. S. T., 115, 204
Quangos, 76
Quermonne, J.-L., 191

Rand Corporation, 73
Ranson, S., 8, 18, 196
Reagan, R., 21, 33, 38, 52, 64, 91, 168
Recruitment, 20, 34
Redwood, J., 32, 76, 204
Rein, M., 14, 29, 204
Reorganization, 17, 96, 98, 150
Representative bureaucracy, 15, 22, 34–37
Research strategies, 108
Richardson, J., 117, 204
Richardson, S. A., 113, 204
Ridley, F. F., 3, 204
Riggs, F. W., 3, 8, 22, 204
Rockman, B. A., 9, 16, 21, 64, 148, 157, 185, 190
Roethlisberger, F. J., 107, 204
Roos, L. L., 113, 204

Roos, N. P., 113, 204
Rose, R., 7, 10, 14, 27, 28, 34, 41, 48, 68, 154, 159, 178, 203, 204, 205
Rosenbloom, D. H., 35, 176, 199, 201
Rothman, S., 205
Rourke, F. E., 165, 205
Rowan, H., 156, 205
Rowat, D. C., 3, 205

Salamon, L., 9, 40, 78, 80, 205
Sanera, M., 21, 192
Savage, P., 8, 205
Savas, E. S., 40, 205
Scandinavia, 117, 172–74, 175
Schain, M. A., 206
Scharpf, F. W., 18, 196
Schmidt, K. D., 205
Schmitter, P. C., 40, 205
Schnapper, D., 73, 87, 100, 101, 102, 193
Schwartz, R. D., 207
Scott, W. R., 62, 64, 191
Sechrest, L., 207
Seidman, H., 17, 62, 72, 86, 92, 201, 205
Self, P., 4, 205
Senegal, 15
Senior Executive Service (U.S.), 39
Sharkansky, I., 9, 17, 27, 96, 104, 205
Siedentopf, H., 204
Siffin, W. J., 8, 194, 205
Sigelman, L., 132, 205
Simon, H. A., 4, 23, 62, 116, 123, 205
Sjoberg, G., 20, 110, 205
Sloman, A., 19, 148, 155, 208
Smallwood, F., 21, 114, 201
Smith, B. C., 8, 18, 203
Smith, B. L. R., 47, 195, 196, 197, 200
Smithburg, D. W., 62, 205
Socialization, 16, 112, 117

Index

Social science theory, 1, 2, 8, 18, 22, 24, 40, 148, 165, 181, 182, 188
Social Security, 52, 76
Social structure, 20, 36
Spain, 22
Spann, R. M., 58, 122, 127, 130, 205
Staber, U. H., 77, 200
Stahl, I., 127, 206
Ståhlberg, K., 147, 169, 200, 206
Stanbury, W. T., 118, 206
Standard and Poor, 42, 206
Stanley, J. C., 109, 192
Starbuck, W., 82, 85, 89, 202
State governments (U.S.), 116, 132
State theory, 40
Statistiska Centralbyrån, 55, 206
Statsföretags AB (Sweden), 32
Straw, B., 190
Steinkemper, B., 173, 206
Steinman, M., 196
Stern, I., 47, 206
Stevens, A., 157, 168, 206
Stevenson, W., 85, 201
Stone, D., 77, 206
Street-level bureaucrats, 15, 20, 110, 111
Stupak, R. J., 147, 152, 201
Suleiman, E. N., 10, 19, 37, 109, 153, 173, 175, 185, 200, 204, 205, 206
Sunset laws, 92
Superbureaucrats, 174–75
Sveriges Statskalendar (Sweden), 73, 74, 101, 103
Sweden, 20, 32, 33, 53–55, 73–75, 100–103, 157, 172, 174
Swierczek, F. W., 23, 194
Szablowski, G., 19, 109, 151, 152, 175, 185, 192, 206
Szanton, P., 205
Szoboszlai, G., 196

Tait, A. A., 15, 38, 197
Tarschys, D., 40, 73, 79, 206
Tax evasion, 115–16

Tax policy, 45, 50
Taylor, C. L., 203
Termination, 81, 82, 83, 90–91, 94–99, 103
Thatcher, Margaret, 30, 31, 38, 158
Third-party government, 9, 17, 27, 72, 78
Third World, 14
Thompson, D. L., 203
Thompson, V. A., 62, 205
Top Salaries Review Body (U.K.), 135
Training, 169, 172–74
Transfer payments, 46
Treasury (U.K.), 16, 19, 109, 125, 128, 151, 175, 176
Tullock, G., 57, 119, 126, 167, 206, 207
Tummala, K. K., 3, 207

Udy, S., 23, 145, 207
United Kingdom, 17, 19, 20, 25, 43, 69–70, 72, 105, 108, 125, 130–32, 135, 148, 149, 154, 158, 161, 168, 172, 174
United States, 1, 2, 4, 6, 17, 20, 25, 39, 42, 51, 79–100, 103, 105, 117, 128–29, 131, 133–35, 149, 152, 168, 175, 184
U.S. Bureau of the Census, 49, 134, 137, 207
U.S. Department of Agriculture, 62–64, 69, 86
U.S. Department of Defense, 42, 49, 73, 81, 139, 207
U.S. Department of Education, 157
U.S. Department of Housing and Urban Development, 64, 66–67, 69, 140
U.S. Department of Labor, 49, 53, 194, 207
U.S. Government Manual, 17, 64, 85, 86, 87, 103
University Grants Committee (U.K.), 30
University of Strathclyde, 34

Index